CHRISTMAS Boosters

Celebrate the Spirit of Christ Through Christmas Traditions

Brent R. Evans

Christmas Boosters

Celebrate the Spirit of Christ Through Christmas Traditions

115 Christmas Traditions and Ideas

Brent R. Evans—Learning Success

www.learningsuccess.com

Bookwise Publishing

Riverton, Utah

bookwisepublishing.com

References from the New Living Translation (NLT) of the Bible

Library of Congress Control Number: Pending

ISBN 978-1-60645-202-8 Paperback

11 23 2018 version

TABLE OF CONTENTS

CELEBRATE THE SPIRIT OF CHRIST

The beginning of a good attitude is gratitude,
because appreciation increases the value
of everything in your life.
There is no faster way to build an abundance of joy
than to increase your appreciation of all that you have.

PREFACE

A Joyful Christmas Season

I am listening to the *Nutcracker Suite* as I attempt to put into words an epiphany I had regarding *Christmas Boosters*. One of the definitions of *epiphany* is the manifestation of Christ to the gentiles as represented by the Magi in Matthew 2: 1–12. Later the word meant an experience of sudden and striking realization or a moment of sudden and great revelation or insight. This is what I experienced. My epiphany.

I thought of the phrase, *Merry Christmas*, and what it means and how deeply it is connected with joy. I suddenly started celebrating the thought as I realized how much more it encompasses. Part of *Merry Christmas* means having positive courage and joyful faith in being in full favor with Jesus Christ. Now, connect that with joy. Jesus Christ said:

> I have told you these things
> so that you will be filled with my joy.
> Yes, your joy will overflow!
>
> —John 15: 11

Yes! Your joy will overflow! Imagine your joy overflowing and realize it is a priceless gift you can have.

> I have come that they (you and I)
> might have life and that they (you and I)
> might have it more abundantly.
>
> —John 10:10

We can have life more abundantly!

Joy is the wonderful experience we have as we fulfill our potential. This is explained beautifully by Rollo May in his book, *Man's Search for Himself.*

But to the extent that we do fulfill our potentialities as persons, we experience the most profound joy to which the human being is heir. When a little child is learning to walk up steps or lift a box, he will try again and again, getting up when he falls and starting over again. And finally, when he does succeed, he laughs with gratification, his expression of joy in the use of his powers. But this is nothing in comparison to the quiet joy when the adolescent can use his newly emerged power for the first time to gain a friend, or the adult's joy when he can love, plan and create. Joy is the effect that comes when we use our powers. Joy, rather than happiness, is the goal of life, for joy is the emotion that accompanies our fulfilling our natures as human beings.

This gives even greater meaning to songs like *Joy to the World.*

The Lord coming and fulfilling His potential to save the world and provide the means whereby everyone can learn and grow to their full potential created such a profound feeling of joy that even the trees clapped. You will go out with joy and be led out in peace.

For ye shall go out with joy,
and be led forth with peace:
The mountains and the hills
shall break forth before you into singing,
and all the trees of the field shall clap their hands.

—Isaiah 55: 12

Christ told us, "Be ye therefore perfect." This instruction is clear and powerful. Who are we? Each of us is a child of Heavenly Father. For us to feel joy to the fullest, we need to fulfill our potential to become more and more like Heavenly Father intended us to be.

Remember, the Kingdom of Heaven is within you. That is where you experience it, and the glory of it is far beyond any material treasure.

The Kingdom of Heaven is like a treasure that a man discovered hidden in a field. In his excitement, he hid it again and sold everything he owned to get enough money to buy the field.

—Matthew 13: 44

Again, the Kingdom of Heaven is like a merchant on the lookout for choice pearls. When he discovered a pearl of great value, he sold everything he owned and bought it!

—Matthew 13: 45-46

The greatest treasure we can find or gift we can possess is being connected to heavenly energy and fulfilling our full potential as children of Heavenly Father. That is where traditions, rituals, and routines come in. Imagine if you greeted each day and each other with the words *Merry Christmas* and be filled with joy.

THE MAGIC OF CHRISTMAS

The magic of Christmas is something we experience individually in the development of our personal relationships with our Savior, with those we love as we glow in this increase of our shared love, and with those to whom we reach out and touch with the love of Jesus Christ. It is a time to hear again the words called out by John the Baptist.

Repent ye: for the kingdom of heaven is at hand . . .
Prepare ye the way of the Lord,
make his paths straight.

—Matthew 2: 2–3

It is a time of cleansing and reordering in preparation for His coming. He came to the world, and we need to receive Him. To do this, our hearts need to be open and not like the innkeeper at Bethlehem, whose inn was too full with other guests to give Him shelter.

Let not our hearts be busy inns,
That have no room for Thee,
But cradles for the living Christ
And His nativity.

Still driven by a thousand cares
The pilgrims come and go;
The hurried caravans press on;
The inns are crowded so!

Oh, lest we starve, and lest we die,
In our stupidity,
Come, Holy Child, within and share
Our hospitality.

Let not our hearts be busy inns,
That have no room for Thee,
But cradles for the living Christ
And His nativity.

—Ralph Spaulding Cushman

Let Him be reborn anew in you, and then the Kingdom of Heaven will truly be at hand, for the Kingdom of Heaven will be within you. Jesus urges us to learn of Him so that we may have Eternal life and find comfort.

I am come that they might have life,
and that they might have it more abundantly.

—John 10: 10

Come unto me, all ye that labour and are heavy laden,
and I will give you rest.
Take my yoke upon you, and learn of me;
for I am meek and lowly in heart:
and ye shall find rest unto your souls.

—Matthew 11: 28–29

Have you pondered the fact that after He was born, Mary laid Him in a manger for you and, throughout His life, He chose to live in humble circumstances that He might reach you more easily? Picture Him washing the feet of His apostles. As you view His life, is it not clear that He will come wherever you are, will meet you in whatever circumstances in which you find yourself, and that if you truly seek Him, He is ready to serve you? You can never be too lowly for His loving care.

As the Spirit of Christ grows within you, celebrate Him, appreciate Him, and make His way straight. Then help Him enter the hearts of other children of God as you bear witness of His divinity to the world. Taking special care for one another is what He wants, especially at this special time, Christmas. Then each of us will celebrate the season in its most perfect ways, whatever our position and circumstances. The rewards for doing so are great, even the kingdom of heaven.

But they that wait upon the Lord,
they shall mount up with wings as eagles.

—Isaiah 40: 31

115 CHRISTMAS TRADITIONS & IDEAS

With this collection of 115 traditions and ideas, you can begin to plan for this Christmas season, or even next Christmas; after all, the New Year celebration is all about goals. Make this one of yours. My family and I hope they are helpful and wish you and your family a very special and merry Christmas.

Merry Christmas!

Brent R. Evans

Of all people on earth, perhaps Christians can most deeply say and appreciate the meaning of the words *Merry Christmas*. The word Christmas refers to Christ and mass—or the Lord's Supper.

It is also called communion. This is the sacramental ordinance churchgoers have the privilege of participating in each week. The Greek equivalent was the word *Eucharist*, meaning returning to good favor or grace. Christmas, then, means returning to full favor with Jesus Christ. Is this not what we do when we partake of the sacrament? All of the scriptures, even from the beginning of this world, point to this ordinance, sacrifice, and gift of Jesus Christ that make it possible.

Over and over again, through thousands of years, sacrifices were made as all of God's people looked forward to the time of the great sacrifice when the Messiah would come to redeem His people. No opportunity was missed to teach and remind His people of the importance of that which was to come. The children of Israel were plagued in the desert by serpents.

The Lord said unto Moses,
Make thee a fiery serpent,
and set it upon a pole:
and it shall come to pass,
that every one that is bitten,
when he looketh upon it, shall live.
And Moses made a serpent of brass,
and put it upon a pole, and it came to pass,
that if a serpent had bitten any man,
when he beheld the serpent of brass, he lived.

—Numbers 21: 8–9

Centuries later, the Apostle John wrote . . .

And as Moses lifted up the serpent in the wilderness,
even so must the Son of man be lifted up:
That whosoever believeth in him should not perish,
but have eternal life.
For God so loved the world,
that he gave his only begotten Son,
that whosoever believeth in him should not perish,
but have everlasting life.
For God sent not his Son into the world to condemn the world;
but that the world through him might be saved.

—John 3: 14-17

To teach Abraham, and through him us, what that love meant, God asked him to sacrifice his and Sarah's only son, Isaac. Can you imagine, even now, what dread Abraham must have felt?

The hand of Abraham was stopped at the last moment, and Isaac was spared. But our Heavenly Father so loved the world, and Jesus so loved us, that His sacrifice was completed and His gift was given to us all.

During this season, we often say to each other, "Merry Christmas." The word merry in Old English meant a special kind of cheer based on courage and faith—the type of joy that the angel must have felt as he announced this to that small group of shepherds outside on the hills surrounding Bethlehem.

Fear not: for, behold, I bring you good tidings of great joy.

—Luke 2: 10

Have you ever noticed in the title of the song, *God Rest Ye Merry, Gentlemen*, that there is a comma between *Merry* and *Gentlemen*? It is not calling them *Merry Gentlemen*; we miss so much of the beauty of this song if we ignore that simple comma. A better reading would be this . . .

God [give you joyful faith], gentlemen,
let nothing you dismay,
Remember Christ our Savior
Was born on Christmas Day;
To save us all from Satan's power
When we were gone astray.
O tidings of comfort and joy, comfort and joy;
O tidings of comfort and joy.

Is any merry? Let him sing psalms.

—James 5: 13

And it is so lovingly expressed by Paul . . .

Be filled with the spirit;
Speaking to yourselves in psalms and hymns and spiritual songs,
singing and making melody in your heart to the Lord.

—Ephesians 5: 18–19

As we shake each other's hands and wish each other a *Merry Christmas*, in its deepest meaning, we are saying, "Have positive courage and joyful faith in your being reconciled and in good favor with Jesus Christ." Isn't that a wonderful and special thing to be able to say to each other? Let us say it to each other often. *Merry Christmas!*

Celebrate the spirit of Christ more deeply during the Christmas season and throughout the year. In addition to these ideas, directions are included. for activities, scripture and other quotations, and stories to go with the traditions and ideas to enrich your holiday experiences.

Merry Christmas

thankful
GRATEFUL
AND
blessed

1. Start Christmas on Thanksgiving

As we feel gratitude and thanksgiving, our hearts will open up to the beauty outside ourselves, and we will become more teachable to the Spirit. So, what better time could there be than Thanksgiving to start celebrating the Christmas season? If our hearts are receptive, we can truly plan to have the best Christmas ever—not just on Christmas day but also during a season's worth of days as we grow closer to God and become His children here upon the earth.

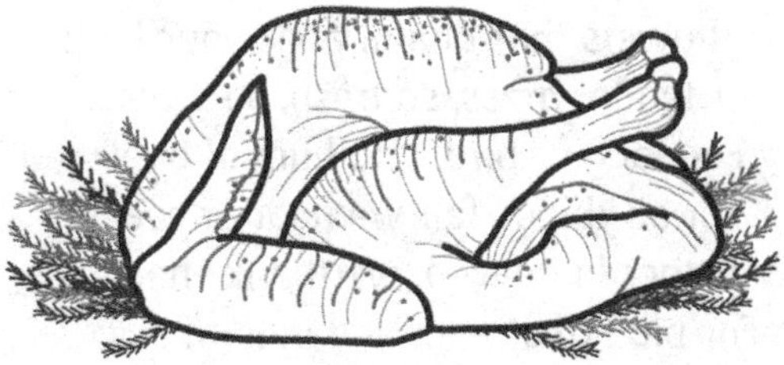

There is something I believe with all of my heart.
It's not a coincidence
that Thanksgiving falls before Christmas on the calendar.
A season of gratitude always prepares
our hearts for a season of giving.

—Emily Freeman

Also, the way the word *thanksgiving* is used in the scriptures and in literature supports the idea that the day we celebrate Thanksgiving is a good time to commit to having a Merry Christmas (positive courage and joyful faith in our being reconciled and in good favor with Jesus Christ).

Enter into his gates with thanksgiving,
and into his courts with praise;
be thankful unto him, and bless his name.

—Psalms 100: 4

Sing unto the Lord with Thanksgiving;
Sing praise upon the harp unto our God:
Who covereth the heaven with clouds,
Who prepareth rain for the earth,
Who maketh grass to grow upon the mountains,
And herb for the use of men.
He giveth to the beast his food,
And to the young ravens which cry.
Praise the Lord, O Jerusalem:
Praise thy God, O Zion.

—Psalms 147: 7–9, 12

For flowers that bloom about our feet:
For tender grass, so fresh, so sweet:
For song of bird, and hum of bee:
For all things fair we hear or see,
Father in heaven, we thank Thee.
For blue of stream and blue of sky;
For pleasant shade of branches high;
For fragrant air and cooling breeze;
For beauty of the blooming trees,
Father in Heaven, we thank Thee.

—Ralph Waldo Emerson

2. Create Your Christmas Bucket List

What kinds of things would you like to do this Christmas season? Do you want to build a snowman? See *The Nutcracker*? Go to a live Nativity? Participate in a *Messiah* Sing-Along?

Gather your family around and create a Christmas bucket list. Post the list on your refrigerator where it is visible and check them off as you complete them. Doing so will help your family get the most out of the season. Find out about scheduled events in your area and add them to your calendar.

3. Appreciate the Many Names & Titles of Christ

Jesus Christ is known by many names and titles, such as the Son of God, the Great Jehovah, the Good Shepherd, and our Advocate with the Father. Each reveals different roles, facets, and attributes of our Savior. As we take time to ponder on each of His names and titles we will gain a greater appreciation and knowledge of His character and who He is to us personally.

Choose and make simple ornaments with the names you will focus on this season. You can do this by decorating and writing on craft sticks or using vinyl lettering on a set of glass ornaments. Be creative.

Take one of the ornaments out each day and place it on the tree. Read the scriptures that go along with that name and discuss how it relates to the Savior, His character, and His relationship with us.

Use the name chosen in your prayers and whenever you refer to the Savior throughout the day.

Below are few to get you started. You can add names that you and your family come up with as well.

Neither is there salvation in any other:
for there is none other name under heaven
given among men, whereby we must be saved.

—Acts 4:12

Alpha and Omega. Alpha is the first letter of the Greek alphabet. We learn from this name that Christ was there from the beginning with the Father before this world was. He is also known as the Omega, being the last letter of the Greek alphabet and used to signify the last, the end, or the ultimate limit. He will be there when the Earth passes away.

I am Alpha and Omega,
the beginning and the end,
the first and the last.

— Revelation. 22:13

I Am. Christ is not only the Alpha and Omega of the vast universe, but He was there from our personal beginning and will be there, always, in our future. But there is more! He is also the Great I AM. He is with us here now, in the present. He is not simply the beginning and the end, He is the beginning through the end. He was there before us, He will be there after us, and if we call upon His name, He will be with us this very minute as an active participant in our lives.

Jesus said unto them,
Verily, verily, I say unto you,
Before Abraham was, I am.

—John 8:58

True Vine. Christ has declared to us that He is the True Vine. What good are the branches if they are not firmly attached to the vine? If we want to bear fruit, and bring good into our lives and into the lives of others, we must "abide in Christ." We must be centered in Him or else, as He so blatantly told us in these verses, we can do nothing.

I am the true vine, and my Father is the husbandman.
Abide in me, and I in you.
As the branch cannot bear fruit of itself,
except it abide in the vine;
no more can ye, except ye abide in me.
I am the vine, ye are the branches:
He that abideth in me, and I in him,
the same bringeth forth much fruit:
for without me ye can do nothing.
If a man abide not in me,
he is cast forth as a branch, and is withered;
and men gather them, and cast them into the fire,
and they are burned.
If ye abide in me, and my words abide in you,
ye shall ask what ye will, and it shall be done unto you.
Herein is my Father glorified,
that ye bear much fruit;
so shall ye be my disciples."

—John 15: 1, 4-8

Door of the Sheep. Knowing that Christ is the door gives special meaning when He entreats us to 'knock and the door shall be opened unto you.'

We can also reason that if we do not ask, we will not receive; if we do not seek, we will not find; and if we do not knock the door will not be opened unto us.

Then said Jesus unto them again,
Verily, verily, I say unto you,
I am the door of the sheep.
I am the door: by me if any man enter in,
he shall be saved,
and shall go in and out,
and find pasture.

—John 10:7,9

Advocate with the Father. An advocate is a person who publicly supports or recommends a particular cause; in this case each one of us. Who better to have in our corner than the Savior of the World?

My little children,
these things write I unto you,
that ye sin not.
And if any man sin,
we have an advocate with the Father,
Jesus Christ the righteous.

—1 John 2:1

Bread of Life. Bread is a basic staple meal and can be synonymous with food. Christ is telling us that he is essential for life. Jesus is not referring to the physical life, but a glorious and joyful eternal life.

And Jesus said unto them,
I am the bread of life:
he that cometh to me shall never hunger;
and he that believeth on me shall never thirst.

—John 6:35

Names of Jesus

Advocate with the Father —1 John 2:1

Almighty —Revelation 1 :8

Alpha and Omega —Revelation 22 :13

Amen —Revelation 3 :14

Apostle —Hebrews 3 :1

Author and Finisher of Our Faith —Hebrews 12:2

Author of Eternal salvation —Hebrews 5:9

Beginning of the Creation of God —Revelation 3:14

Beloved Son of God —Matthew 3:17

Blessed for evermore —2 Corinthians 11:31

Bread of life — John 6: 35

Bright and morning star —Revelation 22: 16

Brightness of God's glory —Hebrews 1: 3

Bridegroom —Matthew 9: 15

Captain of man's salvation —Hebrews 2: 10

Carpenter —Mark 6: 3

Carpenter's son —Matthew 13: 55

Chief Cornerstone —Ephesians 2:20

Chief Shepherd —1 Peter 5: 4

Chosen of God —Luke 23: 35

Christ —Matthew 16:15–16

Creator of Heaven and Earth —Colossians 1: 16–17

Deliverer —Romans 11: 26–27

Door of the Sheep —John 10: 7,9

Exemplar —John 13: 15

First and the last —Revelation 1:17

First fruits of them that slept —1 Corinthians 15: 20

God's Anointed —Acts 4: 27–28

God manifest in the flesh —1 Timothy 3: 16

Good Shepherd —John 10: 11,14

Great High Priest —Hebrews 4: 14

He that liveth and was dead —Revelation 1: 18

Head of the Church —Ephesians 4: 15-16

High Priest of good things to come —Hebrews 9: 11–12

Holy One —Acts 3: 14–15

Hope and Glory —Colossians 1: 27

I Am —John 8: 58

Image of God —2 Corinthians 4: 4

Immanuel —Isaiah 7: 14

Intercessor —Hebrews 7: 25

Jehovah —Isaiah 12: 2

Jesus of Nazareth —Acts 3: 6

Joseph's son —Luke 4: 22

Judge of the quick and the dead —Acts 10: 42

King of Israel —John 12: 12-13

King of Kings —Revelation 17: 14

King of the Jews —Matthew 2: 2

Lamb of God —John 1:29

Light of the world —John 8: 12

Living bread —John 6: 51

Living stone —1 Peter 2: 4

Lord —Luke 2: 11

Lord of Lords —Revelation 17: 14

Lord of peace —2 Thessalonians 3: 16

Master —Matthew 23: 10

Mediator —1 Timothy 2: 5

Messias (Messiah) —John 1: 41

My Lord and my God —John 20: 28

One with the Father —John 10: 30

Only Begotten of the Father —John 1: 14

Rabboni —John 20: 16

Redeemer —Job 19: 25

Resurrection and the Life —John 11: 25–26

Risen Lord —1 Corinthians 15: 3–4

Rock —1 Corinthians 10: 4

Same yesterday, today, and forever —Hebrews 13: 8

Savior —Luke 2: 11

Son of David/Abraham —Matthew 1: 1

Stem of Jesse —Isaiah 11: 1

True vine —John 15:1, 4–8

The way, the truth, and the life —John 14: 6

Word —John 1: 1,14

Wonderful, Councellor, the Mighty God, the Everlasting Father, the Prince of Peace.

—Isaiah 9: 6

He is all these and so much more!

4. Set a Time to Read Scriptures Daily

Reading the scriptures is a way we can visit with our Savior each and every day. It can be done individually, reading silently to yourself, or it could be done with family or friends, reading aloud. Scripture reading invites the Spirit into your home and keeps your family focused on Christ. The following topics and scriptures could be used for this special season of the year.

Who the Lord is.

—Psalms 19 and Hebrews 5: 9

Looking for the Messiah.

—Isaiah 40

Christ's birth.

—Luke 2: 1–20

5. Christmas Wall

Prepare a special bulletin board or a wall on which you can place items. Then look for Christmas themes, thoughts, stories, and pictures to hang up with any Christmas cards you receive from family and friends.

This will be an active project throughout the season and family members will love to see the wall come to life with Christmas treasures. Guests that come into your home will enjoy seeing and learning the significance of the items placed on the wall and may want to contribute their own! They will feel more a welcome part of your life as they spot their card or picture on your wall. They will also know that in your house, you serve the Lord.

Choose you this day whom ye will serve;
but as for me and my house, we will serve the Lord.

—Joshua 24: 15

Nevertheless we, according to his promise,
look for new heavens and a new earth,
wherein dwelleth righteousness.
Wherefore, beloved, seeing that ye look for such things,
be diligent that ye may be found of him
in peace, without spot, and blameless.

—2 Peter 3: 13–14

6. Keep Christmas Simple

Keep Christmas simple enough to feel the spirit of the season and the love of Jesus Christ. Write down your goals for the season, and post this list on your Christmas wall, refrigerator, or mirror to help to keep your priorities clear.

But seek first the kingdom of God,
and his righteousness;
and all these things will be added unto you.

—Matthew 6: 33

European nobility during the Middle Ages had a fortified tower called a keep built within their castles as a place of refuge and of last resort if the castle were to fall under attack by their enemies. Keep that in mind as you read the following scripture:

But Mary kept all these things,
and pondered them in her heart.

—Luke 2: 19

Do we do the same? Do we hold the miracle of Christ's birth in our hearts and ponder on the sacred nature of the Christmas season, or do we run out of time? Do we *keep* Christmas by fortifying the spirit of Christ against the unending distractions and cares of the world? Do we fortify our homes, our time, and our families from missing out on the true spirit of Christmas, the true spirit of Christ?

I will honour Christmas in my heart, and try to keep it all the year.
I will live in the Past, the Present, and the Future.
The Spirits of all Three shall strive within me.
I will not shut out the lessons that they teach.

—*A Christmas Carol* by Charles Dickens

7. Have Your Home Declare Christ

The Spirit of Christ can touch the hearts of others when the way you decorate your home clearly shows that you are celebrating His birth, not just the holiday season.

Some ideas may include collecting or creating your own Nativity sets. It can be a wonderful addition to have one that children can play with. Try embroidering, painting, or using vinyl lettering to display words such as Believe, Joy, Peace in Christ, or O Holy Night that lift thoughts and hearts heavenward.

Decorating your front door with messages or symbols of hope and faith in Christ can greatly influence how people coming in will feel.

Behold, I stand at the door,
and knock:
if any man hears my voice,
and open the door,
I will come in to him,
and will sup with him,
and he with me.

—Revelation 3: 20

I am the door;
by me
if any man
enter in,
he shall be saved,
and shall go
in and out,
and find pasture.

—John 10: 9

Sing praises to the Lord, which dwelleth in Zion:
declare among the people his doings.

—Psalms 9: 11

8. Holiday Foods

Reserve some special foods that you will usually have only at this time of year with your family and friends. You could even create a special Christmas-time recipe book. As you share these special foods, you can remember that feasting together on special holidays has been a long-lasting tradition for the Lord's people.

Thus saith the Lord God of Israel, Let my people go,
that they may hold a feast unto me in the wilderness.

—Exodus 5: 1

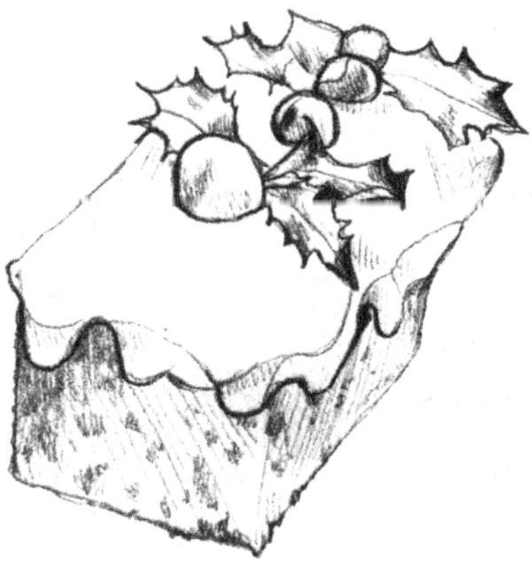

9. Decorate the Table with Purpose

Use special Christmas plates, silverware, tablecloths, or centerpieces that are used only during the Christmas season. A shallow box turned upside down can be used to elevate various Christmas scenes, such as the Nativity. Here are a few ideas for table decorations to try.

- Prepare and use special table decorations that will symbolize the birth of the Savior or a blessing of living the gospel. These can include place mats with pictures of the Nativity or scriptures on them, figurines of the Savior, or various other Christmas decorations that have symbolic meanings such as holly to represent Christ's crown of thorns.
- One year, the table settings might include the scriptures as a centerpiece, with the thought expressed being that we should feast spiritually on the scriptures just as we feast physically on food.
- A practice many years ago was to spread straw on the table, and then cover it with a white tablecloth in memory of Christ's birth in a stable.

These scriptures will encourage you as you prepare this holiday tradition.

Thou preparest a table before me
in the presence of mine enemies:
thou anointest my head with oil;
my cup runneth over.
Surely goodness and mercy
shall follow me all the days of my life:
and I will dwell
in the house of the Lord forever.

—Psalms 23: 5–6

Let not mercy and truth forsake thee:
bind them about thy neck;
write them upon the table of thine heart:
So shalt thou find favour and good understanding
in the sight of God and man.

—Proverbs 3: 3–4

10. Wrap Presents with Love

Plan special ways to wrap and present gifts. The wrapping on the presents can symbolize that they are wrapped in your love and in the Spirit of Jesus Christ. During the weeks before Christmas Day, write loving and caring thoughts on plain wrapping paper for each present. Commitments of service and support to one another could also be written, and name tag stickers or notes may also be attached. Include your testimony of Jesus Christ and your appreciation for His gifts.

Then, as you pass out gifts, the giver may take the gift over to the receiver and read the words written on it and add, "I love you" and wish them a Merry Christmas and a successful New Year in the gospel. This same idea may be used on presents that you send in the mail.

Every good gift and every perfect gift is from above,
and cometh down from the Father of light,
with whom is no variableness, neither shadow of turning.

—James 1: 17

11. Christmas Past, Present, & Future

Put together a binder to use for family Christmas memories and Christmas planning. The binder can be divided up into three books: The book of Christmas past, Christmas present, and Christmases to come.

Christmas Past. Near the beginning of the Christmas season, reminisce about past Christmases and write down some of these stories. Particularly, listen for and write down appreciation statements about acts of love and service that have been experienced. Recording these actions will help you and your family to appreciate these experiences more as a part of your own family's heritage.

Remember the days of old,
consider the years of many generations:
ask thy father, and he will shew thee;
thy elders, and they will tell thee.

—Deuteronomy 32: 7

Christmas Present. Be sure to write down stories, take photos or videos of events that are taking place this Christmas season. When the season comes to a close, include these new items in your *Book of Christmas Past.* As you celebrate in the Spirit of Christ, you will see His loving influence, and your holiday memories will draw you closer to Him.

The original meaning of the word behold involved more than mere looking. It meant to hold fast to or to grasp. Think of ways that you can behold the Spirit of Christ more this holiday and as you read such scriptures as these.

The next day John seeth Jesus coming unto him, and saith,
Behold the Lamb of God, which taketh away the sin of the world.

—John 1: 29

Christmases Yet to Come. Make next Christmas even better and more special. Think about the needs and goals of family, friends, and others and what can be done to help them enjoy the Spirit of Christ even more next year. Write them down so you may refer back to them at the beginning of the next Christmas season. Add them now to next year's holiday schedule.

As you make room in your busy holiday schedule, focus on the Savior and serving one another, and He will bless you and your family.

But whosoever will be great among you,
let him be your minister;
And whosoever will be chief among you,
let him be your servant:
Even as the Son of man came
not to be ministered unto,
but to minister,
and to give his life a ransom for many.

—Matthew 20: 27–28

12. Special Christmas Tree Ornaments

The word ornament has an interesting history that can add to the meaning of placing them on your Christmas tree. It comes from a Latin verb that means to adorn or add beauty. Another early meaning was to set in order, resulting in the related word, ordinance.

Think of hanging ornaments on your Christmas tree; then as the symbolism of adding beauty to life by setting things in order through the ordinances of the gospel. Make and use special Christmas tree ornaments to help you remember this symbolism.

- Each year, place photos of loved ones on ornaments and hang them on the tree. As years go by, your tree will hold more and more memories of love, family, and friendship. Even distant family members could participate by sending photos to each other. Include pictures of your ancestors as a reminder of your eternal bonds. Maybe, on one ornament or sign near the top of the tree, include the following scripture so that it can be seen clearly.

A new commandment
I give unto you,
That ye love one another;
as I have loved you,
that ye also love one another.

—John 13: 34

- Make cookie ornaments in symbolic shapes or with words or pictures illustrating the Spirit of Christ or principles of the gospel.
- Each child could have his or her own personal Christmas ornaments that are packed away between seasons in a box with his or her name on it. Each year, children could choose or receive new ornaments that they can open on Christmas Eve and put on the tree. When the children are grown and start their own homes, they could be given their ornaments with which to start their own Christmas tree.

13. The Meaning of Decorations

Review and do research on the meanings of various Christmas decorations or customs. Here are a few examples:

- Holly and Berries. The holly represents the crown of thorns placed on Jesus just before He was crucified; the berries represent his blood.
- Candles. The candle represents Christ, the light of the world.
- Christmas Tree. The Evergreen symbolizes life in the midst of winter. It points upward to remind us where all good gifts come from.
- A Star. The star atop the Christmas tree represents the star of Bethlehem.
- Lights. The lights on Christmas trees or homes have great symbolic meaning when reading the following poem and scripture.

Hold High the Torch!

Hold high the torch!
You did not light its glow—
'Twas given you by other hands, you know.
'Tis yours to keep it burning bright,
Yours to pass on.
For there are other feet we must guide,
And other forms go marching by our side;
Their eyes are watching every smile and tear
And efforts which we think are not worthwhile,
Are sometimes just the very helps they need,
Actions to which their souls would give most heed;
So that in turn they'll hold it high and say
"I watched someone else carry it this way."

Hold high the torch!
You did not light its glow—
'Twas given you by other hands, you know.
I think it started down its pathway bright,
The day the Maker said: "Let there be light."
And He once said, who hung on Calvary's tree.
"Ye are the light of the world."
Go! Shine for me.

—Anonymous

I am the light of the world:
he that followeth me shall not walk in darkness.

—John 8: 12

Customs from other lands that represent hope and love may also be appreciated as representing the Spirit of Christ throughout the world and during any age.

It is a custom in the Ukraine to hang a spider or web on the Christmas Tree as a symbol of hope. The story goes that the children of a poor widow nurtured the sprouts of a fallen pine cone looking forward to the wonderful prospect of someday having their very own Christmas tree. Finally, the tree had grown big enough to bring into their modest dwelling, but sadly they could not afford to decorate the tree. The spiders, observing their disappointment and sad cries, decided to help. They got to work spinning their webs over the little tree, creating beautiful patterns and designs. The children burst into their mother's room Christmas morning joyfully beckoning, "Come look, Mother! How beautiful!" The mother was overjoyed to see the splendid delicate strands of gold and silver glistening on the tree as the sun shone in their window welcoming a bright new Christmas morning.

14. Christmas Stories

Read a short Christmas story together each night. Choose a special book from which to read each year. Not all of the stories need occur in actual Christmas settings. They just need to uplift our spirits and bring us closer to the love of our Savior. Reading favorite stories could become a tradition as beauty and strength are drawn from them year after year.

The Christmas Carol by Charles Dickens was published in 1843. Its appearance created a national and international rebirth to celebrating Christmas. Read it every Christmas; it may do the same for your family.

Another great story traditionally read and shared at Christmas time is *The Mansion* by Henry Van Dyke. This short book can be read online.

Books! Books! Books!

And we thank Thee, God
For the gift of them;
And the lift of them;
For the gleam in them

And the dream in them;
For the things they teach
And the souls they reach!

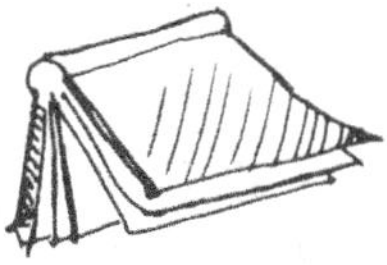

For the maze of them
And the blaze of them;

For the ways they open to us
And the rays that they shoot through us.
Books! Books! Books!
And we thank Thee, God.

For the light in them
For the might in them;

For the urge in them;
And the surge in them.
For the souls they wake
And the paths they break;
For the going in them,
And the song in them;
For the throngs of folk they bring to us,
And the songs of hope they sing to us!

—William L. Stidger

15. Connect with Loved Ones

Set aside a special day to visit or phone family and friends. Find out what is going on in their lives, and tell them how much you appreciate them. Then bear your testimony of Jesus Christ.

What made us friends in the long ago
When we first met?
Well, I think I know;
The best in me and the best in you
Hailed each other because they knew
That always and always since life began
Our being friends was part of God's plan.

—Anonymous

16. Uplift Others

Have a goal of increasing the self-esteem and well being of others by ten percent. Have that be the goal for each encounter even while realizing it may take more encounters before that goal is fully accomplished. For example, you want a cashier to feel ten percent better after you go through his or her line at the grocery store, but your goal will continue each and every time thereafter. You can consider that a very good investment.

Be especially aware of the depressed and help them rise up. Each holiday season, there is an increase in the number of people suffering from depression. Think of ways you may be able to help, and then make a plan to do something kind for someone who may be feeling lonely or downhearted.

Wherefore lift up the hands which hang down,
and the feeble knees.

—Hebrews 12: 12

For if they fall, the one will lift up his fellow.

—Ecclesiastes 4: 9–10

If I can stop one heart from breaking,
I shall not live in vain;
If I can ease one life the aching,
Or cool one pain,
Or help one fainting robin
Unto his nest again,
I shall not live in vain.

—Emily Dickinson

Think of ways that you can comfort and bring hope in the life of someone who has suffered loss. Consider the true story behind the popular Christmas carol, *I Heard the Bells on Christmas Day.*

Henry Wadsworth Longfellow had great reason to sorrow and lose hope. His beloved wife, Fanny died after her dress caught fire in a tragic accident. He, himself, was severely burned and disfigured as he tried to put out the flames by wrapping his arms around her. The Christmas after her death, Henry wrote, "How inexpressibly sad are all holidays. 'A merry Christmas' say the children, but that is no more for me." Not much time would pass before he received a telegram that his son, Charly, was severely wounded in battle as a bullet pierced his shoulder and rounded down to his spine within an inch of leaving him paralyzed. Longfellow wrote, "I can make no record of these days. Better leave them wrapped in silence. Perhaps someday God will give me peace."

On Christmas day 1863, Longfellow wrote these words of when despair turns to hope:

I heard the bells on Christmas day
Their old familiar carols play,
And wild and sweet the words repeat
Of peace on earth, good will to men.

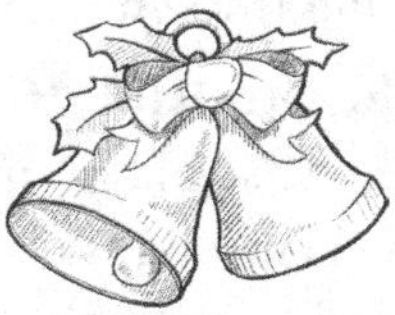

I thought how, as the day had come,
The belfries of all Christendom
Had rolled along th' unbroken song
Of peace on earth, good will to men.

And in despair I bowed my head:
"There is no peace on earth," I said,
"For hate is strong and mocks the song
Of peace on earth, good will to men."

Then pealed the bells more loud and deep:
"God is not dead, nor doth he sleep;
The wrong shall fail, the right prevail,
With peace on earth, good will to men."

Till, ringing, singing, on its way,
The world revolved from night to day,
A voice, a chime, a chant sublime,
Of peace on earth, good will to men.

17. A Joyous Christmas Party

At your next holiday get-together, play some games that help people to get to know and appreciate one another better. Here are two games you can try.

- **Story Ball.** Players sit in a circle. A timer is set. Then one player holds a ball and starts telling a story. At a point of his or her choice, this player suddenly tosses the ball to someone else, who must catch the ball and continue the story without hesitation. The game continues with the ball being thrown back and forth to various players until the time runs out.
- **The Minister's Cat.** Players sit in a circle and clap a steady rhythm. The first player names a letter and then, in time with the rhythm of the clapping, says, "The minister's cat is a ________ (descriptive word starting with that letter) cat." For example, if the letter in play is c, the player might say, "The minister's cat is a cute cat." Then the next player must continue without missing a clap and use another adjective starting with the same letter to describe the cat. Any player that is unable to think of a new word or keep up with the rhythm is out. In that case, the next player may start with a new letter of his or her choice. The game continues until only one player, the winner, is left. Try it with different statements. "The meal tonight was a ______ meal." "Dad's new car is a _____ car." "Sister's new boyfriend is a_______ boyfriend.

Plan a fun theme for your gathering. Here are some ideas:

- **Ugly Sweater.** Always a favorite, how about an ugly sweater contest? See who can create the absolute worst sweater or sweatshirt. Use real Christmas lights and ornaments. And then get a panel of judges and give prizes. This can be a blast and makes for great photos for the picture books!
- **Fezziwig's Ball.** Hang the mistletoe, get out the plum pudding, and move the furniture out of the way to make room for games and merry dancing!

- **Cheesy Mug Party.** Have guests bring their cheesiest mugs and enjoy a hot chocolate bar with whip cream, marshmallows, candy canes, cinnamon, flavorings, and sprinkles.
- **Feliz Navidad.** Tacos, maracas, a Christmas piñata, and heaps of Hispanic flare. You can even decorate a Christmas cactus to display. Play Spanish guitar music and observe Hispanic Christmas customs such as illuminating the walkways with small candle lanterns.

Laughter is Like Sunshine

A laugh is just like sunshine,
It freshens all the day,
It tips the peak of life when light,
And drives the clouds away;
The soul grows glad that hears it,
And feels its courage strong;
A laugh is just like sunshine
For cheering folks along.
A laugh is just like music,
It lingers in the heart,
And where its melody is heard,
The ills of life depart;
And happy thoughts come crowding
Its joyful notes to greet;
A laugh is just like music
For making living sweet.

—Anonymous

18. Gifts You Can't Wrap

Consider whether five dollars or one hour of service would do the most good. Then try this experiment. Review the needs of people you know. Spend five dollars in a way that meets a need or two, then spend one hour of your personal time or attention to meet a need or two. Which made the most difference?

Because service blesses the lives of both the giver and the receiver, providing gifts of loving service can invite the Spirit of Christ into your holiday celebrations better than spending money on gifts ever could.

May God forbid that we should present our gifts
and withhold ourselves.

—Anonymous

Who gives himself, with his alms, feeds three:
Himself, his hungering neighbor, and me.

—The Vision of Sir Launfal by James Russell Lowell

19. Add to Your Nativity Set Each Year

Start a nativity set that will have a new piece added each year. Begin with the baby Jesus and His mother, Mary. Add Joseph the following year, a shepherd the year after, and so on. Each Christmas Eve, or on another specific evening, present the new piece to your family and share the significance and meaning of the new chosen piece and how it has place in your nativity set. The first several years will be easy as you go through the important events in the Christmas story, but who or what else could be found surrounding the manger and honoring the Christ child in future years?

20. Track Your Children's Growth

If you have growing children or grandchildren, mark each one's height on a garage wall each year. During that same time, discuss and write down each child's growth in learning and living the gospel of Jesus Christ.

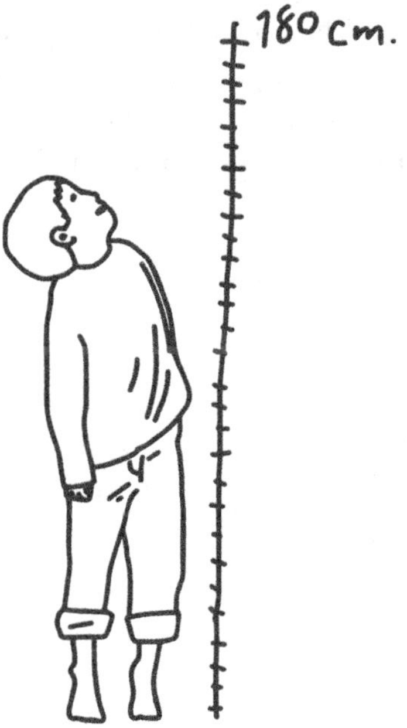

And Jesus increased
in wisdom and stature,
and in favour with God and man.

—Luke 2: 52

Till we all come into
the unity of the faith,
and of the knowledge
of the Son of God,
unto a perfect man,
unto the measure
of the stature
of the fullness of Christ.

—Ephesians 4: 13

21. Christmas Cookies & Cakes

Prepare cookies or cakes and decorate them with symbolic pictures or Christmas words on them. Then share these with family and friends to remind them of Christ's birth.

Organize a cookie pool. Set aside a day when friends and family can bake cookies in their own homes. Put all the cookies into a common pool from which they can draw out their share of a variety to take home and enjoy.

Connect this experience with the commandment to be one in Christ. Good things happen when we share our talents. Then, with a prayer, ask the Lord to bless the cookies so they may remind your family that they are truly brothers and sisters in God's family.

O taste and see that the Lord is good:
blessed is the man that trusteth in him.

—Psalms 34: 8

O renew us, Lord, we pray,
With thy Spirit day by day,
That we ever one may be
With the Father and with thee.

—William Wordsworth

This is my commandment,
that ye love one another, as I have loved you.

—John 15: 12

22. Books Under the Tree

Children's books have a magical way of shaping children into who they will become. Start a collection of wonderful and faith promoting children's Christmas books and stories that you can add to each year. Wrap them under the tree for your children to open each night before bedtime. The books and the messages they contain can truly be gifts that you give to your child. They will feel your love for the Savior and gain a testimony of showing kindness and compassion to others as you read through the pages.

You can find magic wherever you look.
Sit back and relax, all you need is a book!

—Dr. Seuss

23. Family Chain Caroling

Schedule a night for chain caroling where one family starts by caroling another family. Then that family is invited to join the first family in going to another family's house to carol them. The third family is also invited by the group to go to the fourth family, and so on. You could finish the evening with cookies and hot chocolate.

The French word for Christmas carol was *noel* and originally meant a cry of joy. So, before you go out caroling, review the story of the ark of the covenant of the Lord with your family. Tell them about the joy the people felt when it was brought by David to the capital, Jerusalem. The people had been without the ark for many years, and now, it was finally in their midst again.

FA la LA

So David, and the elders of Israel,
and the captains over thousands,
went to bring up the ark of the covenant of the Lord
out of the house of Obededom with joy.
And it came to pass,
when God helped the Levites
that bare the ark of the covenant of the Lord,
that they offered seven bullocks and seven rams.
And David was clothed with a robe of fine linen,
and all the Levites that bare the ark, and the singers,
and Chenaniah the master of the song with the singers:
David also had upon him an ephod of linen.
Thus all Israel brought up the ark of the covenant
of the Lord with shouting,
and with sound of the coronet,
and with trumpets, and with cymbals,
making a noise with psalteries and harps.

— 1 Chronicles 15: 25–28

Singing music which praises and honors the Savior invites His Spirit and brings us closer to Him, filling our hearts with joy.

Sing unto him, sing psalms unto him,
talk ye of all his wondrous works.
Glory ye in his holy name:
let the heart of them rejoice that seek the Lord.

—1 Chronicles 16: 9–10

24. Art Museums & Concerts

Experience how artists and composers have tried to capture the Spirit of Christ through religious themes. If you can't visit museums or attend concerts in person, they can be experienced online. Many concerts are available to watch in your own living rooms through streaming services. Explore art online and in books or take virtual museum tours online.

25. Christmas Treasure Hunt

Visit your public library as a family. Ask everyone to explore available items with Christmas themes. Then gather together the books, audio recordings, and videos that seem interesting and uplifting. Finally, return home and share some of the ideas you found.

And ye shall seek me, and find me,
when ye shall search for me with all your heart.

—Jeremiah 29: 13

26. Scripture Advent

Traditionally, an Advent calendar provides twenty-four openings that can each be accessed separately, one day at a time, for each day before Christmas, beginning with December 1st. If you are beginning your family's Christmas season on Thanksgiving, though, you may want to add more openings for the extra days in November.

Make your Advent house out of two layers of paper or cardboard. Design it so that it has doors cut into the top layer for all of the days. Behind each door, write a scripture on the bottom layer that you would like to memorize. Open one door each day, and try to have that scripture memorized before the end of the day. You could even make it a goal to have all these scriptures memorized by Christmas Day.

Search the scriptures;
for in them ye think ye have eternal life:
and they are they which testify of me.

—John 5: 39

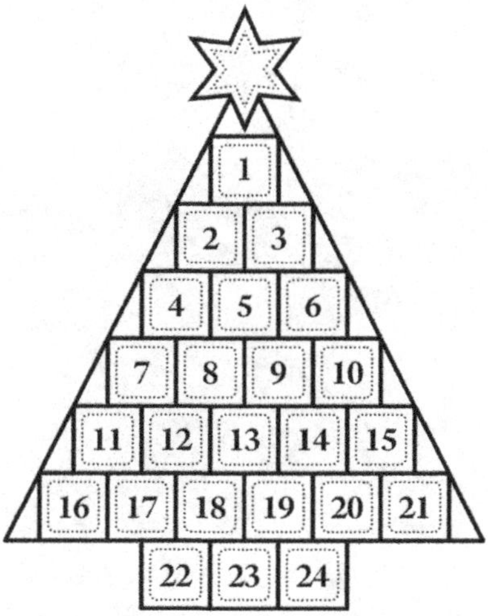

27. A Light in the Window

This tradition, dating back many years in Ireland, was to put a candle in the window on Christmas Eve. To some, this candle was lit so the Christ child could find His way to that house in the night. To others, the light was meant as a welcome sign to strangers in need.

Decorate one of your windows and include a safe light source, like an LED candle or a strand of Christmas lights. Then share the following beautiful poem from that era with your family:

On Christmas Eve a candle light
To shine abroad through Christmas night,
That those who pass may see its glow,
And walk with Christ a mile or so.

—Carolyn Sherwin Bailey

28. Decorate the Tree Party

Hold a special party of family and friends to decorate each other's Christmas trees. Go to the homes of people living alone or in need of assistance and help them to decorate theirs. Plan a party later, when the Christmas tree is ready to be taken down to help put the decorations away.

As you do this, include promises of love and devotion to each other and to the gospel through the year on small notes. This will help your Christmas tree be an important symbol of joy at the birth of the Savior. Then read the following scriptures after each tree is decorated:

For ye shall go out with joy,
and be led forth with peace:
the mountains and the hills
shall break forth before you into singing,
and all the trees of the field shall clap their hands.

—Isaiah 55: 12

Let the heavens be glad,
and let the earth rejoice:
and let men say among the nations,
The Lord reigneth.
Let the sea roar,
and the fullness thereof:
let the fields rejoice,
and all that is therein.
Then shall the trees of the wood
sing out at the presence of the Lord.

—1 Chronicles 16: 31–33

29. Bless Christmas Dinner

Establish the tradition of having a special Christmas Day blessing on the food at dinnertime. Before the prayer, invite each person to contribute thoughts to include. This will help you to make it a true group prayer. Then the group's spokesperson can include those thoughts in the prayer. They might also want to take notes on the group's contributions before the prayer is offered.

Again I say unto you,
That if two of you shall agree on earth
as touching any thing that they shall ask,
it shall be done for them
of my Father which is in heaven.

—Matthew 18: 19

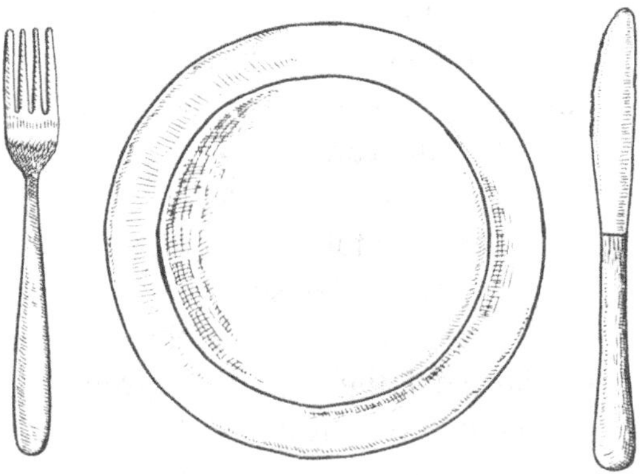

30. Bedtime Carols

Listen to a different Christmas carol each night just before saying your nightly prayer and going to bed. Christmas thoughts will help create a peaceful and warm rest.

Thou wilt keep him in perfect peace,
whose mind is stayed on thee.

—Isaiah 26: 3

This scripture is even more descriptive and meaningful when we realize that the word stayed refers to the ropes and stays used to hold a ship's mast upright, even in terrible storms. When our minds are filled with thoughts tied to our Savior's birth, the Spirit of Christ will support and strengthen us to face any challenge or difficulty.

31. Host a Christmas Music Dance

Dancing is a means of expression of joy, a way to focus our feelings, and an enjoyable way to associate with people. Planning a time to dance to Christmas music can be a special way to celebrate the season as a family or group of friends. Did you know that the early meaning of the word carol meant to dance in a ring while singing? Thus, carols originally were meant to be danced to.

Praise ye the Lord. Sing unto the Lord a new song,
and His praise in the congregation of saints.
Let Israel rejoice in Him that made him:
let the children of Zion be joyful in their King.
Let them praise His name in the dance:
let them sing praises unto Him with the timbrel and harp.
For the Lord taketh pleasure in His people:
He will beautify the meek with salvation.

—Psalms 149: 1–4

32. Lovely Thoughts Night

Gather quotations, poems, proverbs, artwork, music, stories, scripture references, etc., whatever represents or generates beautiful thoughts and feelings. Spend time enjoying these lovely things by yourself or with others. Note that beauty comes from the Lord and from following His teachings, and then read these scriptures:

> He hath made every thing beautiful in his time . . .
>
> —Ecclesiastes 3: 11

> Give unto the Lord the glory due unto his name;
> worship the Lord in the beauty of holiness.
>
> —Psalms 29: 2

33. Christmas Shows & Musical Performances

Listen to and see special holiday movies, musical performances, or presentations. Choose programs for your family to enjoy that enhance the meaning and deepen your appreciation of Christmas. Attend special Christmas programs at local churches, even those not of your faith. Watch *Mr. Krueger's Christmas* on YouTube.com. It's excellent.

> Mr. Krueger examined the small Nativity scene on his table and began to think so hard of its meaning that he felt himself actually there, adoring the Christ baby. Love flowed from his heart as he recounted what the Lord meant to him.

Listen to *The Messiah* by George Frideric Handel. Written over 200 years ago, it is still a powerful force today in proclaiming the Savior to the world at Christmas. The story behind how it was written is as remarkable and inspiring as the music itself.

> George Handel was at a low point in his music career. He had suffered major physical ailments and was getting on in years, so his music was becoming less popular, and he was facing financial difficulties.
>
> He often walked the streets at night in his depression. Then, one late night, he arrived home and saw on his table a manuscript of an oratorio that had been left there by a then insignificant poet. As he read some of it, Handel came across words about Jesus Christ that struck his soul.

He was despised and rejected of men . . .
He looked for someone to have pity on him,
but there was no man;
neither found He any to comfort Him . . .
He trusted in God . . .
He will give you rest . . .
I know that my Redeemer liveth . . .
Rejoice . . . Hallelujah.

Suddenly, it was as if the entire composition of music for The Messiah was playing in George's mind. He worked feverishly for twenty-three days and nights to get it written, neglecting his need for food or rest. When he finished writing the triumphant climax to the Hallelujah Chorus, with tears in his eyes, he told his servant, "I did think I did see all Heaven before me and the great God, Himself!"

Later, when the last note was written, Handel collapsed on his bed and slept for seventeen hours. His servant finally called for the doctor, but George awoke before the doctor arrived and was found fully refreshed and eating a hearty meal. He dedicated the proceeds of all performances of *The Messiah* to the Foundling Hospital.

In one performance in London, the King of England was so moved by Handel's music during the *Hallelujah Chorus* that he stood up and remained standing until its conclusion. The people in the audience also stood up which remains a tradition to this day.

Handel lived another seventeen years and, although he ran into other misfortunes in life, including going blind, his spirit remained strong. At age 74, at a performance of *The Messiah*, he collapsed and was taken home. He announced, "I should like to die on Good Friday." He died on April 14, 1759, which was just one day after Good Friday and the anniversary of the first presentation of *The Messiah*.

34. Inspirational Christmas Journal

Use a small journal and record beautiful thoughts and scriptures. Review them every Christmas season, and add to them each year. Ask friends and family to gather together to add to your journals. Then family and friends can bring some of their favorite beautiful thoughts or quotes to share with each other as gifts during the Christmas season. This can become a way of adding beautiful thoughts to each others' books to help focus on the Spirit of Christ during the holiday.

> The beautiful spoken word can be heard and treasured in the heart, but the actual words may dim over time. That is where the written word, also treasured in the heart, can step in to keep the words forever in a state of perfect freshness. Consider your life to be a bouquet of flowers made up of all your lovely thoughts and experiences.
>
> —Brent R. Evans

> By his spirit he hath garnished the heavens.
>
> —Job 26: 13

35. Visit a Sacred Place

Visit a church, synagogue, temple, or any place you consider sacred and where you can spend time pondering and listening to the spirit. This can even be an especially beautiful place in nature or a place of personal significance. It is important to schedule time away from the stresses and distractions of the world to truly commune with God.

Using one of the previously mentioned activities before or following your visit can help create that extra spirituality and depth of feeling that can make a difference in your life.

Some early morning, go to your sacred place with your family and watch the sunrise. Dawn's light represents how each new day can bring a beautiful rebirth of Christ within you and a new opportunity to serve Him. Later, have breakfast together, and invite others to share their thoughts.

One thing have I desired of the Lord that will I seek after;
that I may dwell in the house of the Lord all the days of my life,
to behold the beauty of the Lord, and to inquire in his temple.

—Psalms 27: 4

36. Christmas Oranges

There is nothing so sweet, fragrant, fresh and delightful as an orange. Throughout most of history, having an orange to enjoy was rare and considered a luxury. For so many, it was a treat savored only once a year . . . Christmas morning! Children would wake Christmas morning to find the anticipated treasure hidden in a stocking with a few candies and nuts, or they would eagerly run across the street, knock on a neighbor's door and say, "Christmas Orange!" upon which the juicy citrus would be bestowed.

There is a beautiful Christmas movie entitled *Christmas Oranges* (2012) that would be meaningful to watch together with your family.

During the Christmas season, keep a bowl of fresh oranges out for family and friends to enjoy.

You may want to follow a Colonial American holiday tradition and make orange clove pomanders that will fill your home with a wonderful Christmas aroma. Simply, fill an orange with whole cloves by piercing a desired pattern into the skin of the orange with a toothpick or skewer and placing whole cloves into the premade holes. If desired, you can tie a ribbon around the orange to hang it on the tree. The sweet scent of the orange pomander will last the entire year.

37. Christmas Testimony Meeting

Set aside a time for testimony sharing on Christmas Day, possibly just before exchanging presents or just before or after Christmas dinner. Mention the appreciation you have felt for the blessings you have received because of Jesus Christ.

Ye are my witnesses, saith the Lord . . .
ye may know and believe me,
and understand that I am he . . .
I, even I, am the Lord;
and beside me there is no saviour . . .
Ye are my witnesses, saith the Lord, that I am God.
—Isaiah 43: 3–12

38. State of the Family Address

Establish the tradition of having the matriarch or patriarch of the family prepare and give a State of the Family address. This might include family members' accomplishments, new marriages, births, moves, new jobs, life changes, interesting projects, health concerns, and the needs of individuals within the family. Conclude with hopes and wishes for the family's future.

Life is a country that the old have seen and lived in.
Those who have to travel through it can only learn the way from them.

—Joseph Joubert

Age is opportunity no less than youth itself,
though in a different dress,
and as the evening twilight fades away,
the sky is filled with stars, invisible by day.

—Henry Wadsworth Longfellow

39. Family Post Office or Information Center

Establish a central email, Google doc, or other shared information center with extended family. Begin with two: one for the mother's parents and descendants, and one for the father's parents and descendants.

Initiate a family project to collect the names, addresses, phone numbers, emails, and birth dates for everyone. When this is finished, email each household a copy of the complete list. Every year during the Thanksgiving weekend, have each household prepare an email to the family, or write notes or letters and actually mail them from the post office! It's fun to get mail, but especially to have the handwriting of your extended family. Just a paragraph or two about their family's current activities and status along with a Christmas greeting is all that is needed, but you might find some real nuggets added in by some of the fine writers in your family groups. Do this every year and send them out to everyone on the mailing list to keep in touch and feel close even when far apart.

Those who are absent, by its means become present;
it (mail) is the consolation of life.

—Voltaire

40. Make Room for Mary & Joseph

Set aside a part of your home for Joseph and Mary that can represent your willingness to take them in when they were seeking shelter at the inn. If this requires some sacrifice, it will work even better as a teaching and learning experience. Imagine they are really coming to stay with you, then prepare it, knowing for whom you are providing the accommodations.

Spend time in this place to ponder the significance of what Mary and Joseph knew was about to take place nearly 2000 years ago in Bethlehem. On Christmas Eve, go there and read aloud the story of the birth of the Savior as recorded in Luke. Sing a few Christmas carols. As you do, the Spirit of Christ will increase your understanding of their meaning to you, personally, and to all the world.

And she brought forth her firstborn son,
and wrapped him in swaddling clothes,
and laid him in a manger;
because there was no room for him in the inn.

—Luke 2: 7

41. Christmas Appreciation

Each day in December, set aside time to write about things you appreciate or incidents where other people showed you special consideration or love. Also, recall people in your past who showed love for you, and try to express the appreciation you still feel for those people and the love they gave you.

As you write each day, something almost magical will happen: you will begin to remember and appreciate more things as you dip into the treasures that reside within you, patiently waiting to be rediscovered. The beginning of a good attitude is gratitude, because appreciation increases the value of everything in your life. There is no faster way to build an abundance of joy than to increase your appreciation of all that you have.

Sing unto the Lord with thanksgiving.

—Psalms 147: 7

And to stand every morning to thank
and praise the Lord, and likewise at even.

—1 Chronicles 23: 30

42. Do Unto Others

Explore in your own mind how you would like others to act toward you. Write this down in as much detail as possible. Include specific examples. Then, for one week, make a valiant effort to treat others in those same ways.

If you are doing this as a family or as a group of friends, select a particular week for the project, but do not reveal the ways you have decided to act until the end of the week. Then, take time to allow each person to share what he or she was trying to do and how it felt to obey Christ's instruction.

Therefore all things whatsoever ye would that men should do to you, do ye even so to them: for this is the law and the prophets.

—Matthew 7: 12

43. Christmas Quilts

Organize a project in your family to make a collective Christmas quilt. Ask everyone to make one new quilt block. Even family members living a great distance away can mail their blocks to keep them at a central location where they may be assembled. Do this every year until you have enough for a large quilt, or make a variety of small ones. Just as the pieces of the quilt are sewn together in one, your family can be one in purpose and unity and one in Christ.

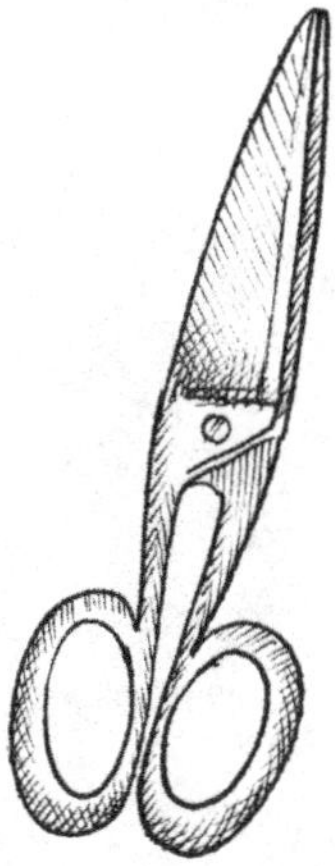

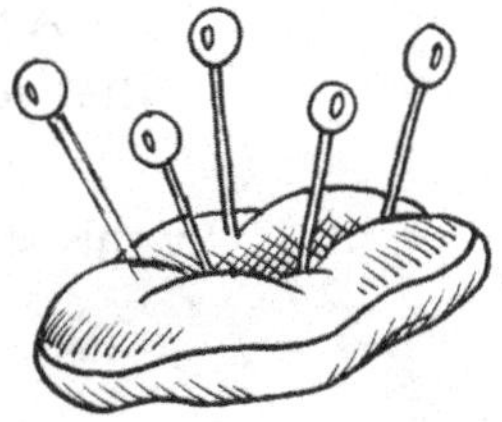

My life is but a weaving
Between my Lord and me.
I cannot choose the colors
He worketh steadily.
Oftentimes he weaveth sorrow,
And I in foolish pride
Forget He sees the upper
And I, the underside.
Not till the loom is silent,
And the shuttles cease to fly,
Shall God unroll the canvas
And explain the reason why.
The dark threads are as needful
In the Weaver's skillful hand
As the threads of gold and silver
In the pattern He has planned.

—Author Unknown

44. Sharing Time

Set aside a time with family or friends to sit in a circle and give each one a liberal amount of time to share what is going on in their lives—perceptions, goals, interests, fears, needs, etc. After everyone has had enough time to share, encourage them to give each other gifts of care and love by expressing love, offering support for their goals, and committing to help them in meeting the needs or fears that were revealed earlier.

A new commandment I give unto you,
That ye love one another; as I have loved you,
that ye also love one another.
By this shall all men know that ye are my disciples,
if ye have love one to another.

—John 13: 34–35

45. Pictures and Messages for Grandparents

Ask grandchildren to draw pictures and write messages on sheets of paper. Then, deliver or email them to grandparents who may then place them on a special wall. Children can also do this for any elderly people in your area as a way of showing their love at Christmas.

Children may also do other arts and crafts. Certainly, the love that young children are able to express is especially significant during this time of year.

Blessed be childhood,
which brings down something of heaven
into the midst of our rough earthliness.

—Henri Frédéric Amiel

Children, well we know them, never weary
Of their innocent surprise;
Waiting, watching, listening always
With full hearts and tender eyes,
While our little household angels,
Bright and golden in the sun.
Greet us with the sweet old welcome—
"Merry Christmas, everyone!"

—Anonymous

But Jesus said, Suffer little children, and forbid them not,
to come unto me: for of such is the kingdom of heaven.

—Matthew 19: 14

46. A Birthday Cake for Our Savior

To help young children relate to the birth of the Savior, bake and decorate a special birthday cake to be eaten on Christmas Day.

Invite your family to bring gifts for baby Jesus by writing down a service they will do for others and wrapping it up as a present to be opened after cutting and eating the cake. This will help your family, young and old, to feel the joy that comes from serving the Lord and celebrating His birth.

And it came to pass, that,
when Elisabeth heard the salutation of Mary,
the babe leaped in her womb;
and Elisabeth was filled with the Holy Ghost:
And she spake out with a loud voice, and said,
Blessed art thou among women,
and blessed is the fruit of thy womb.
And when is this to me,
that the mother of my Lord should come to me?
For, lo, as soon as the voice of thy salutation sounded in mine ears,
the babe leaped in my womb for joy.

—Luke 1: 41–44

47. Christmas Poster Night

Give each person or team a sheet of paper and some paints, crayons, or colored markers. Then challenge them to make a poster that would represent the spirit of Christmas. When they are finished, display these posters for the rest of the Christmas season or give the posters out to friends or family as loving messages during the Christmas season.

Rings and jewels are not gifts,
but apologies for gifts.
The only gift is a portion of thyself.

—Ralph Waldo Emerson

48. Hang Attribute Socks as Stockings

Help your family members to make attribute socks to use as their Christmas stockings. Each one should choose a word for their sock or stocking, indicating their best righteous quality or qualities they desire to develop during the coming year. Then, each year, everyone considers the new qualities they may have developed or wish to develop and adds words to represent those. On Christmas Eve, explain that the good things they will receive in their stockings represent the blessings that come from living righteous lives.

Couldst thou in vision see
Thyself, the person God meant,
Thou never then would be
The person thou art, content.

—Anonymous

49. Music & Scripture in the Car

Play scriptures and spiritual Christmas music when you are in your car during the Christmas season to feel the Spirit of Christ every day. Look out and appreciate the beauty of the world and of God's children.

Music has a great impact on how you feel and your attitude. Just as food takes on the flavors of the marinade, the things you surround yourself with will sink in and add flavor to your spirit.

O renew us, Lord, we pray,
With thy Spirit day by day,
That we ever one may be
With the Father and with thee.
—William Wordsworth

50. Have a Very Present Christmas

Live in the present moment. What is the most important thing happening right now? Consider the following story:

Now it came to pass, as they went,
that he entered into a certain village:
and a certain woman named Martha received him into her house.
And she had a sister called Mary,
which also sat at Jesus' feet, and heard his word.
But Martha was cumbered about much serving,
and came to him, and said,
Lord, dost thou not care that my sister hath left me to serve alone?
Bid her therefore that she help me.
And Jesus answered and said unto her,
Martha, Martha, thou art careful
and troubled about many things:
But one thing is needful:
and Mary hath chosen that good part,
which shall not be taken away from her.

—Luke 10: 38-42

Mary was cumbered about much serving. She was being productive and doing much good, but she was missing Christ being there.

Be careful this Christmas season not to be cumbered about with less important things. Determine the thing that is needed in the present and chose that good part.

Preparing for Christmas
is more than getting your house ready.
It's getting your heart ready.

—Brent R. Evans

Today

I shall do so much in the years to come.
But what have I done today?
I shall give out gold in pricely sum.
But what did I give today?
I shall lift the heart and dry the tear
I shall plant a hope in the place of fear
I shall speak with words of love and cheer.
But what have I done today?
I shall bring to each lonely life a smile
But give to truth a greater birth
And to steadfast faith a deeper worth.
I shall feed the hungering souls of earth.
But whom have I fed today?

—Anonymous

51. Service Without Payback

Look for things you can do for people who can never pay you back. Then plan and perform some act of service as a family where it can make a difference.

For I was an hungered, and ye gave me meat:
I was thirsty, and ye gave me drink:
I was a stranger, and ye took me in:
Naked, and ye clothed me:
I was sick, and ye visited me:
I was in prison, and ye came unto me.
Then shall the righteous answer him,
saying, Lord, when saw we thee an hungered,
and fed thee? or thirsty, and gave thee drink?
When saw we thee a stranger,
and took thee in? or naked, and clothed thee?
Or when saw we thee sick,
or in prison, and came unto thee?
And the King shall answer and say unto them,
Verily I say unto you,
Inasmuch as ye have done it unto one of the least
of these my brethren, ye have done it unto me.

—Matthew 25: 35–40

But . . . whosoever will be great among you,
let him be your minister;
And whosoever will be chief among you,
let him be your servant:
Even as the Son of man came
not to be ministered unto,
but to minister,
and to give his life a ransom for many.

—Matthew 20: 27–2

52. Share Special Messages

Write Christmas letters to your family and loved ones. Express your love and appreciation for each and bear your testimony of Jesus Christ. It is becoming more and more popular to send family newsletters each year to help loved ones catch up on the year's events and to share in their family's tidings of joy.

The world is waiting for somebody,
Waiting and watching today;
Somebody to lift and strengthen,
Somebody to shield and stay.
Do you thoughtfully question, "Who?"
'Tis you, my friend, 'tis you.

—Anonymous

Create a personal audio or video message to send to your family members or friends. It could contain personal news, stories, messages, music, etc. You could also personalize it so that each person you are sending it to feels greeted and included.

We get from people what we give;
We find in them what we bring;
We discover that the changes in them
Are really changes in ourselves.

—Anonymous

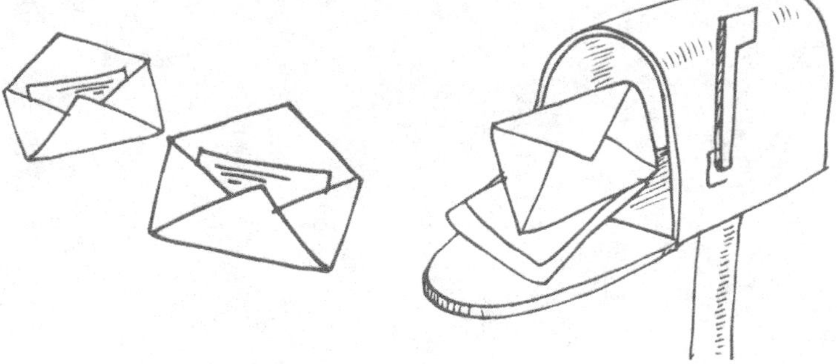

53. Plan to Keep Christmas Through the Year

Get a calendar for next year. As you gather with family and friends, talk about what keeping the spirit of Christmas throughout the year means to each of you. As new ideas come up, write them on the calendar. If an idea applies to a specific day, write the idea there. If it is an idea that you may want to act on anytime during the month, write it in an open space near the name of the month.

Wait on the Lord, and keep his way, and he shall exalt thee.

—Psalms 37: 34

54. Dedicate Your Home for Christmas

Write a prayer of dedication, put it in a frame, and place it on the wall. Make it a tradition to write a new prayer each year. Save the old ones, and read them as a remembrance of past Christmases.

Bless this house, O Lord, we pray,
Make it safe by night and day;
Bless these walls, so firm and stout,
Keeping want and trouble out;
Bless the roof and chimneys tall,
Let thy peace lie over all;
Bless this door, that it may prove
Ever open to joy and love.

—Helen Taylor

55. Take Off Your Shoes

Set aside one day during the Christmas season to express your recognition of the sacredness of your home when it is dedicated to the purposes of the Lord. Demonstrate this by taking off your shoes inside your home. Then invite others to do the same.

And he said, Draw not nigh hither:
put off thy shoes from off thy feet,
for the place whereon thou standest is holy ground.

—Exodus 3: 5

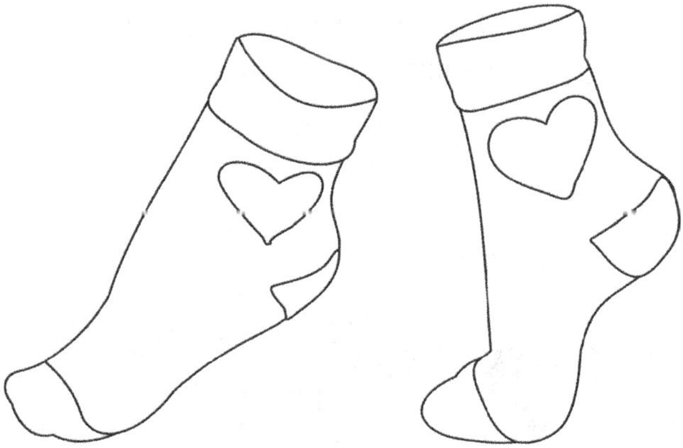

56. Set Your Life by Christ

We need to do more than learn from each other. We need a standard or perfect example. Take time to read about the life of Jesus in the New Testament. Then, read the following story and scripture, and renew your commitment to follow Him.

> There was once a jeweler who had a large clock in front of his shop. He noticed that, day after day, a certain man would stop by his shop and check his watch. One day, the jeweler decided to go out and talk with the man and inquire about this habit. When asked about it, the man said he was in charge of blowing the noon whistle at the town factory and wanted to make sure his watch was correct. The jeweler, somewhat amused, then had to tell the man that he had set his own clock by the noon whistle at the factory.

Jesus saith unto him, I am the way, the truth, and the life:
no man cometh unto the Father, but by me.

—John 14: 6

57. Expand Your Circle

Consider your current friends and associates. Now, think of one or more people you would like to include in your circle. Even consider someone who has seemed unfriendly to you in the past. Go out of your way to reach out, show love, and serve that person.

He drew a circle that shut me out—
Heretic, rebel, a thing to flout.
But love and I had the wit to win;
We drew a circle that took him in.

—Edwin Markham

But love your enemies,
and do good, and lend,
hoping for nothing again;
and your reward shall be great,
and ye shall be the children of the Highest.

—Luke 6: 35

58. The Animals' Christmas

Take one day to pay special attention to the wellbeing of God's creatures. The love that you expend on them will return to you many fold, for all life has a part in God's plan and love.

But ask now the beasts, and they shall teach thee;
and the fowls of the air, and they shall tell thee:
Or speak to the earth, and it shall teach thee:
and the fishes of the sea shall declare unto thee.
Who knoweth not in all these that the
hand of the Lord hath wrought this?
In whose hand is the soul of every living thing,
and the breath of all mankind.

Job 12: 7-10

A righteous man regardeth the life of his beast.

—Proverbs 12: 10

Whence Comes This Rush of Wings?

Whence comes this rush of wings afar,
Following straight the Noel star?
Birds from the woods in wondrous flight,
Bethlehem seek this Holy Night.
"Tell us, ye birds, why come ye here,
Into this stable, poor and drear?"
"Hast'ning we seek the newborn King,
And all our sweetest music bring."
Hark how the Greenfinch bears his part,
Philomel, too, with tender heart,
Chants from her leafy dark retreat,
Re, mi, fa, sol, in accents sweet.
Angels and shepherds, birds o' the sky,
Come where the Son of God doth lie;
Christ on earth with man doth dwell,
join in the shout "Noel, Noel.

—a French carol by Bas Query

59. Behold the Beauty of the World

Take one day to fully appreciate not only the beauty of the world in its natural state, such as the sky, the stars, the mountains, and flowers, but also the beauty created by the sons and daughters of God on the earth. As you appreciate the beauty in God's creations around you, know also that beauty must be within you.

Though we travel the world over to find the beautiful,
we must carry it with us or we will find it not.

—Ralph Waldo Emerson

To him all life was Beauty.
The sun upon the hills.
The sweeping shadows, and the winding lane.
Morning, he loved, with dewdrops on the flowers;
Evening, with sunset and soft, warm April rain.
Friends he found in lepers stumbling to him,
Love in those who hate, grace in sinners' eyes.
Dawn he saw with all earth's new-born glory,
Twilight and darkness, and hope in human sighs.

Youth was his, and springtime, and music in the trees;
Life was his, and sunshine, and the murmuring of bees;
Joy in healing broken hearts; manhood's noble strife;
All the wonder and the beauty of a sacred human life.
He walked the common lanes, the city streets he trod,
And in his heart was Beauty . . .the Beauty born of God.

—Author Unknown

The little cares that fretted me,
I lost them yesterday
Among the fields above the sea,
Among the winds at play;
Among the lowing of the herds,
The rustling of the trees,
Among the singing of the birds,
The humming of the bees.
The foolish fears of what may pass,
I cast them all away
Among the clover-scented grass,
Among the new-mown hay;
Among the hushing of the corn
Where drowsy poppies nod,
Where ill thoughts die and good are born,
Out in the fields with God.

—Author Unknown

60. A Car Parade to Proclaim Christ's Birth

Decorate your cars in ways that announce Christ's birth and have a parade to announce to the world their joy. Honk your horns to proclaim the Christmas season and His birth. Combine it with caroling, or as you go from home to home for a progressive dinner, even on Christmas Day.

Praise ye the Lord.
Praise God in his sanctuary:
Praise him in the firmament of his power.
Praise him for his mighty acts:
Praise him according to his excellent greatness.
Praise him with the sound of the trumpet:
Praise him with the psaltery and harp.
Praise him with the timbrel and dance:
Praise him with stringed instruments and organs.
Praise him upon the loud cymbals:
Praise him upon the high sounding cymbals.
Let every thing that hath breath
Praise the Lord.
Praise ye the Lord.

—Psalms 150

Ye are the light of the world.
A city that is set on an hill cannot be hid.
Neither do men light a candle, and put it under a bushel,
but on a candlestick;
and it giveth light unto all that are in the house.

—Matthew 5: 14–15

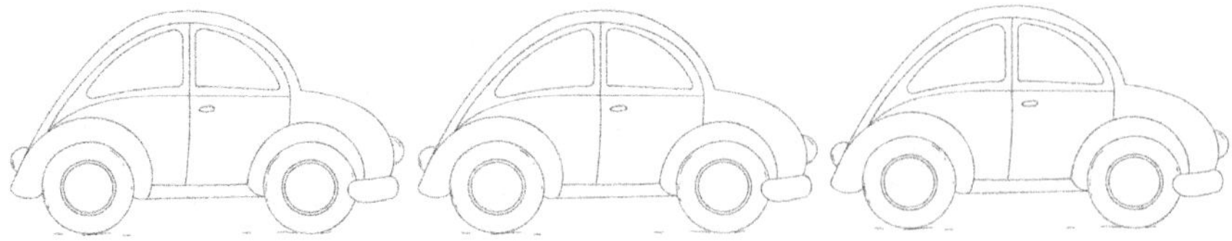

61. Extended-Family Calendar

Each year, prepare an extended-family calendar that includes birthdays, anniversaries, and other important dates. Include family pictures for each month. Add photos of your ancestors. Make your calendar by hand, paste your images onto a purchased calendar, or use a low-cost computer program to design one. There are also online companies that can make these for you. Family photos may be printed or copied in color to protect the originals and share them with everyone.

Working together to create the calendar will build extended-family closeness and love, while the calendars themselves will remind everyone throughout the year of the importance of these eternal relationships.

Where we love is home,
Home that our feet may leave,
but not our hearts.

—Oliver Wendell Holmes

62. Awaken to Words of Joy

Wake up and greet members of your family on Christmas morning with these words of Isaiah.

Arise, shine: for thy light is come,
and the glory of the Lord is risen upon thee.

—Isaiah 60: 1

Make every morning feel like Christmas. Think back to a time in your life when you were genuinely excited to wake up in the morning—to catch an early flight for a vacation you had been anticipating for months; or your first day at a new job, the first day of school, your wedding day, or birthday. I can't think of any time in my life when I was more excited to wake up than when I was a child, every year on Christmas morning.

Your first ritual that you do during the day
is the highest leveraged ritual, by far,
because it has the effect of setting your mind
and setting the context for the rest of your day.

—Eben Pagan

Imagine being connected to an infinite source of loving energy, finally being whole, happy, content, and experiencing life as a source of limitless creative possibility.

63. Special Christmas Morning Service

On your own, or with your family, have a special Christmas service the first thing Christmas morning. This may include a prayer, a song, a talk, and a testimony. Keep it short, but consider how this activity can help generate a special spirit throughout the day. Then, remember this service during the coming year, and draw from its strength each morning as you say a prayer and ponder spiritual things before starting the day. Invite your family to do the same.

Follow up with a special breakfast!

Every morning lean thine arms awhile
Upon the window sill of heaven
And gaze upon thy Lord.
Then, with vision in thy heart,
Turn strong to meet thy day.
— Anonymous

64. Christmas Memory Walks

Gather together and share stories of past Christmases as you take a walk with one another. Discuss how simple things make such big contributions to our lives and our fond memories. Record the stories from each Christmas Memory Walk and save them as a family heritage.

Two or three minutes—two or three hours,
What do they mean in this life of ours?
Not very much if but counted as time,
But minutes of gold and hours sublime,
If only we'll use them once in a while
To make someone happy—make someone smile.
A minute may dry a little lad's tears,
An hour sweep aside trouble of years.
Minutes of my time may bring to an end,
Hopelessness somewhere, and bring me a friend.

—Anonymous

65. Invite the Spirit with Scripture

At the start of the holiday season, challenge yourself and your family and friends to select and memorize favorite verses from the scriptures that will invite the Spirit of Christ into your celebrations. Before opening presents or before partaking of Christmas dinner, ask each family member to read or say from memory one of these favorite and appropriate scriptures.

Man shall not live by bread alone,
but by every word that proceedeth out of the mouth of God.

—Matthew 4: 4

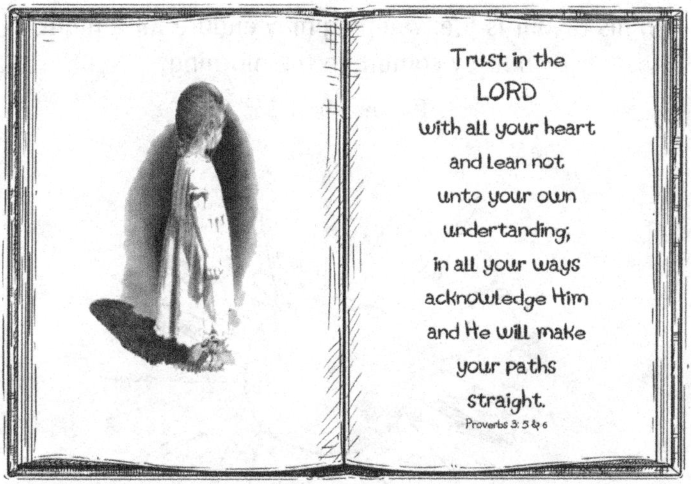

66. I Will See You in the Morning

I will see you in the morning! This is a phrase we often hear and speak, but it can have special meaning this Christmas season and always when you consider that Christ suffered and died so that we might live again. Because of His sacrifice, no matter what happens between now and sunrise, we truly will see our loved ones in the glorious morning. Feel the joy of that knowledge as you make it a habit to always leave your loved ones with the comforting words, "I will see you in the morning."

Sing unto the Lord, O ye saints of his,
and give thanks at the remembrance of his holiness.
For his anger endureth but a moment;
in his favour is life: weeping may endure for a night,
but joy cometh in the morning.

Psalms 30: 4-5

67. Christmas Action Chain

Extend your efforts to feel the Spirit of Christ past Christmas Day, and keep it throughout the coming year. Cut out strips of paper to start your Christmas Action Chain.

Decide on one action you will take during or after Christmas to invite the Spirit of Christ into your heart, perhaps a visit to someone who is sick, or bring a bouquet of flowers for an elderly widow, or a young one. It doesn't matter what you pick, as long as it is in keeping with the Spirit of Christ.

Write that first thing down on a strip of paper. This is the start of your Christmas Action Chain. Don't write down anything else until you have accomplished this one link.

When you have completed this action, date the strip of paper, staple its ends together to form a loop, and then decide on another action. Write this second action down on another strip of paper. Do it, date it, and then wrap it through the first link before stapling it into a loop. Continue with each new action, making the loops into a chain.

See how far you can extend this chain, link by link, throughout the year. With each good action, more spiritual power will come into your heart to motivate you to continue on to the next action. Maybe you can even continue to extend the chain into the next Christmas season.

You may want to read *The Christmas Carol*, by Charles Dickens, just before writing down your first action. Write the following words on a piece of paper as a reminder. Scrooge says them after he rediscovers the joy of Christmas.

I will honor Christmas in my heart and try to keep it all the year.

—Scrooge

68. Throw Away Sorrows, Fears, & Troubles

Just before opening your Christmas presents, ask each person to write down any sins, sorrows, fears, troubles, or grievances they currently have on a blank card. Ask participants to share what they have written, or this information could remain private.

Discuss the meaning of Christmas and the importance of Christ's birth. Ask each person to tear up their card and throw its pieces into a garbage bag. An alternative is, if you have a fireplace, toss them in and burn them along with the traditional Yule log.

Another idea is to use pine cones to represent what you are throwing away. Explain that pine cones are really seedpods. As you throw them into the fire, they will make a beautiful, glowing representation of how throwing away our sins, sorrows, fears, troubles, and grievances can improve our lives.

Follow this activity with hugs all around and rejoicing. Then open presents and enjoy the day in the Spirit of Christ.

Come unto me, all ye that labour,
and are heavy laden, and I will give you rest.
Take my yoke upon you, and learn of me;
for I am meek and lowly in heart:
and ye shall find rest unto your souls.
For my yoke is easy, and my burden is light.

—Matthew 11: 28–30

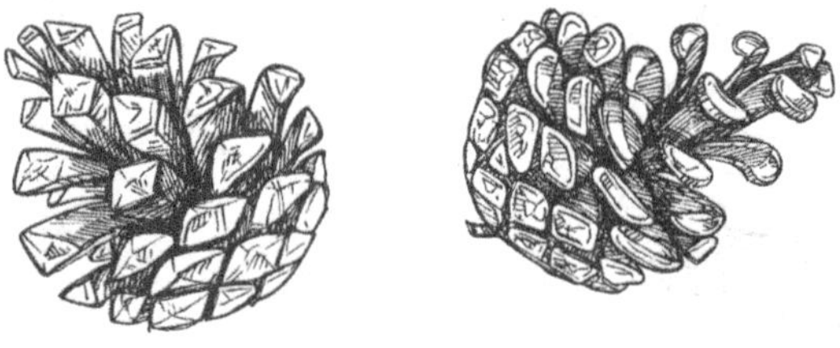

69. Walk Where Jesus Walked

Walk where Jesus walked without having to go to the Holy Land. Accomplish this by doing things He would do wherever you are.

I have given you an example,
that ye should do as I have done to you.

—John 13: 15

To the naked, He is clothing.
To the cold, enduring warmth.
To the hungry, He is food.
To the lonely, a true friend.
To the weak, He is strength,
To the hopeless, a sure way.
To the sick, He is comfort.
To those afraid, a secure guard.
You will find Him wherever there is need.

—Brent R. Evans

If we are to have the very best Christmas ever,
We must listen for the sound of sandaled feet.

—Thomas S. Monson

70. Consider Santa a Messenger of Christ

Each family can have its own beliefs about Santa. The name Kris Kringle evolved from the German Christkind, or Christ Child, or messenger from the Christ Child. When transferred into Pennsylvania Dutch, this name became Christ Kindl or Kriss Kindle. At some point, an r was added, and a d became a g, thus it became Kriss Kringle.

The point is that we can consider Santa Claus, Kris Kringle, Father Christmas, or St. Nicholas as messengers of the Christ Child. Is there a real Santa Claus? Certainly, just look around you, and you can see this fact for yourself.

My father and mother were Santa Claus to me. They were able to bring the Spirit of Christ to me each Christmas. Even now, I can simply think about it, and the wonders of Christmas unfold again in my mind and heart.

You can be a Santa Claus by sharing the Spirit of Christ with others. Anyone can. The word Santa comes from the word saint, meaning one who is pure in heart. You could explain to little children in your family that Santa is someone who knows that Jesus loves the little children and that, as a gift to Jesus on His birthday, Santa tries to make them happy. When your children are old enough, let them be a Santa for a family in need.

I used to believe in Santa Claus.
Then I didn't believe
in Santa Claus.
Now I am one.

—Brent R. Evans

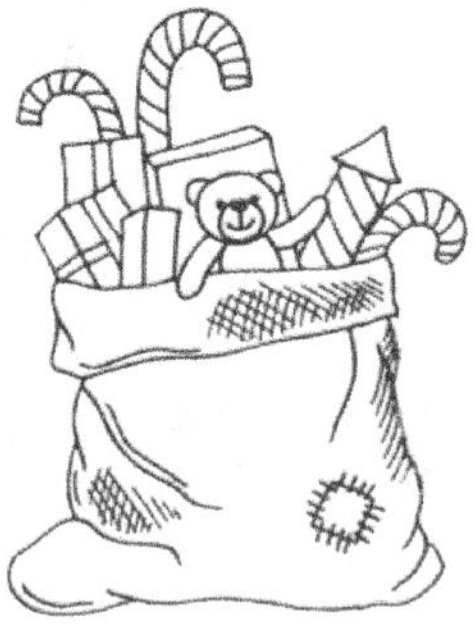

On Christmas Eve
the other night
I saw the most amazing sight,
for there beneath
the Christmas tree
was Santa kneeling
on his knee.

His countenance was different than
that all-familiar, jolly grin;
his head was bowed, and hand to breast,
and slightly tucked into his vest.
For there in a Nativity
was Jesus and His family,
and as I heard him start to pray,
I listened close to what he'd say.
"Lord, You know that You're the reason
I take pleasure in this season.
I don't want to take Your place,
but just reflect Your wondrous grace.
I hope You'll help them understand
I'm just an ordinary man,
who found a way to do Your will
by finding kids with needs to fill.
But all those centuries ago,
There was no way for me to know,
that they would make so much of me,
and all the gifts beneath the tree.
They think I have some hidden power
granted at the midnight hour.
But it is my love for You
Inspiring all the things I do.
And they give You all the Glory,
For, 'You're the One True Christmas Story.'"

—Alda Monteschio

But when he saw the multitudes,
he was moved with compassion on them,
because they fainted, and were scattered abroad,
as sheep having no shepherd.
Then saith he unto his disciples,
The harvest truly is plenteous, but the labourers are few;
Pray ye therefore the Lord of the harvest,
that he will send forth labourers into his harvest.

—Matthew 9: 36–38

71. A Day for Quiet Reflection

Take time to pray and to compare your life with that of a true follower of the gospel of Jesus Christ. Write your thoughts in a journal, and make a list of actions or changes needed. Use the list during the coming weeks and months as you partake of the sacrament each Sabbath. As you make this list, eliminate cares and interruptions of the outside world so your soul may be nourished freely by the Spirit of Christ. On that day, avoid being distracted by TV, electronic devices, newspapers, business, and work. Keep conversations to a minimum, and whisper to show it is a special day for your soul.

Create in me a clean heart,
O God, and renew a steadfast spirit within me.

—Psalms 51: 10

Grant us grace to see thee, Lord,
Mirrored in thy holy word;
May we imitate thee now,
And be pure, as pure art thou.

—William Wordsworth

If ye abide in me, and my words abide in you,
ye shall ask what ye will, and it shall be done unto you.

—John 15: 7

72. Christmas Card Album

Starting and maintaining a Christmas card scrapbook album will allow you and your family to enjoy the Christmas photos and messages again and again throughout the years.

Add comments of your own about the people who sent the cards, such as identifying who they are, sharing any interesting stories about them, and including words of appreciation for what they have meant to you in your life. As you do so, you will feel the Spirit of Christ, and this album will become quite a heritage item for your family to enjoy in the coming years.

At Christmas
the season
of giving and sharing,
of living and loving,
remembering, caring—

Our thoughts
bridge the space that
would tend to divide us,
restoring the warmth of
Your presence beside us.

May all the sweet magic
of Christmas conspire
to gladden our hearts
and fill every desire.

—Harold H. Bennett

73. Christmas Trees by Mail

Make foldout Christmas trees for your family and friends. Draw a Christmas tree shape that when folded in half lengthwise, will fit inside your envelopes.

For each tree, cut out three identical tree shapes, and then fold each in half, creasing along the fold. Place the first shape flat and open. Place the other two tree shapes on top and tape together at the folds so the finished tree may be opened into a three-dimensional tree.

Write personalized sentiments inside for each recipient and use these instead of Christmas cards to send to your loved ones. Do this activity as a family to enjoy sharing the little Christmas trees with one another, taping them up on your Christmas wall.

The Christmas tree, the fairest tree,
On earth no rival knowing;
However small the garden be,
All radiant blooms the wondrous tree,
With every flower glowing…

—German folk song

74. Watch for the First Star

Make a new family tradition to spot the first star to appear in the Christmas Eve sky. At dusk, bundle everyone up, and go outside together. Tell your family that you will count this first star as if it were the new star that appeared at Jesus' birth, the signal that starts Christmas Day.

You might also want to have special treats available, like hot chocolate, to keep people warm as you sing songs together and bear testimonies while you are waiting for the first star to appear. Tell your family that you will all make a joyful shout when you see it.

After your joyful shout, explain that the Jewish day starts at sunset, so Christmas Day has now actually begun. Finally, complete this tradition by having an adult read aloud the following song of joy.

Behold, God is my salvation;
I will trust, and not be afraid:
for the Lord Jehovah is my strength and my song;
he also is become my salvation.
Therefore with joy shall
ye draw water out of the wells of salvation.
And in that day shall ye say,
Praise the Lord, call upon his name,
declare his doings among the people,
make mention that his name is exalted.
Sing unto the Lord; for he hath done excellent things:
this is known in all the earth.
Cry out and shout, thou inhabitant of Zion:
for great is the Holy One of Israel
in the midst of thee.

—Isaiah 12: 2–6

75. Silent Night, Holy Night

Sit quietly where you can see the stars. This might be outside, if it is warm enough, or inside, by a window in your home if you have a good view from there, or even from inside your car. The important thing is to find a place where you can be comfortable and warm so that you can really take in the meaning of that most holy of nights when the Savior was born. Consider the stars as if they were lights on Heaven's Christmas tree that covers the entire earth. Then read and ponder this verse.

The heavens declare the glory of God:
and the firmament sheweth his handy work.

—Psalms 19: 1

Afterward, sing *While Shepherds Watched Their Flocks by Night*, to feel the Spirit of Christ in your quiet celebration, as well.

While Shepherds Watched Their Flocks by Night

While shepherds watched their flocks by night,
All seated on the ground,
The angel of the Lord came down,
And glory shone around.
"Fear not," said he, for mighty dread
Had seized their troubled mind;
"Glad tidings of great joy I bring
To you and all mankind.

"To you, in David's town, this day
Is born, of David's line,
The Saviour, who is Christ the Lord,
And this shall be the sign:
"The heavenly babe you there shall find
To human view displayed,
All meanly wrapped in swaddling bands,
And in a manger laid."

Thus spake the seraph; and forthwith
Appeared a shining throng
Of angels, praising God, who thus
Addressed their joyful song:
"All glory be to God on high,
And to the earth be peace:
Good will henceforth from
Heaven to men
Begin and never cease."

—Nahum Tate

76. Christmas Season Fast

Set aside a day for a special Christmas fast. This means more than just refraining from eating until evening of that day. Contemplate fully those around you who need a servant of the Lord to attend to their needs. Then have a simple meal and reflect on the importance of taking care of people in need.

Connect your special fast with a Christmas carol about good King Wenceslas. Ponder the fact that, in comparison to others of God's children, you are rich. Then sing and have it remind you from this time forward of your own responsibilities to those in need.

Good King Wenceslas

Good King Wenceslas looked out
On the Feast of Stephen,
When the snow lay round about,
Deep and crisp and even;
Brightly shone the moon that night,
Though the frost was cruel,
When a poor man came in sight,
Gathering winter fuel.

"Hither, page, and stand by me,
If thou knowest it, telling:
Yonder peasant, who is he?
Where and what his dwelling?"
"Sire, he lives a good league hence,
Underneath the mountain,
Right against the forest fence,
By Saint Agnes's fountain."

"Bring me flesh, and bring me wine,
Bring me pine logs hither;
Thou and I will see him dine
When we bear them thither."
Page and monarch forth they went,
Forth they went together;
Through the rude wind's wild lament
And the bitter weather.

"Sire, the night is darker now,
And the wind blows stronger:
Fails my heart, I know not how,
I can go no longer."
"Mark my footsteps, my good page,
Tread thou in them boldly:
Thou shalt find the winter's rage
Freeze thy blood less coldly."

In his master's steps he trod,
Where the snow lay dinted;
Heat was in the very sod
Which the saint had printed.
Therefore, Christian men, be sure,
Wealth or rank possessing,
Ye who now will bless the poor,
Shall yourselves find blessing.

Another way to reflect on the importance of taking care of people in need is to connect your special Christmas fast with *The Little Match Girl,* a story told by Hans Christian Andersen. Only the last half of the story is given here, but a little girl was out late at night in the freezing cold without shoes or a proper coat, trying to sell matches during the holiday season. No one bought from her, though, and so she huddled against a wall to try to keep warm.

The Little Match Girl

Her little hands were almost benumbed with the cold. Ah! A match might do her good, if she could only draw one from the bundle, and rub it against the wall, and warm her hands at it. She drew one out. R-r-atch! how it sputtered and burned! It was a warm bright flame, like a little candle, when she held her hands over it; it was a wonderful little light! It really seemed to the little girl as if she sat before a great polished stove, with bright brass feet and a brass cover. How the fire burned! How comfortable it was! But the little flame went out, the stove vanished, and she had only the remains of the burned match in her hand.

A second was rubbed against the wall. It burned up, and when the light fell upon the wall it became transparent like a thin veil, and she could see through it into the room. On the table a snow-white cloth was spread; upon it stood a shining dinner service; the roast goose smoked gloriously, stuffed with apples and dried plums. And what was still more splendid to behold, the goose hopped down from the dish, and waddled along the floor, with a knife and fork in its breast to the little girl. Then the match went out, and only the thick, damp, cold wall was before her. She lighted another match. Then she was sitting under a beautiful Christmas tree; it was greater and more ornamented than the one she had seen through the glass door at the rich merchant's. Thousands of candles burned upon the green branches, and colored pictures like those in the print shops looked down upon them. The little girl stretched forth her hand toward them; then the match went out. The Christmas lights mounted higher. She saw them now as stars in the sky: one of them fell down, forming a long line of fire.

"Now someone is dying," thought the little girl, for her old grandmother, the only person who had loved her, and who was now dead, had told her that when a star fell down a soul mounted up to God.

She rubbed another match against the wall: it became bright again, and in the brightness, her grandmother stood clear and shining, mild and lovely.

"Grandmother!" cried the child, "Oh! Take me with you! I know you will go when the match is burned out. You will vanish like the warm fire, the warm food, and the great, glorious Christmas tree!"

And she hastily rubbed the whole bundle of matches, for she wished to hold her grandmother fast. And the matches burned with such a glow that it became brighter than in the middle of the day; grandmother had never been so large or so beautiful. She took the little girl in her arms, and both flew in brightness and joy above the earth, very, very high, and up there was neither cold, nor hunger, nor care—they were with God.

But in the corner, leaning against the wall, sat the poor girl with red cheeks and smiling mouth, frozen to death on the last evening of the Old Year. The New Year's sun rose upon a little corpse! The child sat there, stiff and cold, with the matches, of which one bundle was burned. "She wanted to warm herself," the people said. No one imagined what a beautiful thing she had seen, and in what glory she had gone in with her grandmother to the New Year's Day.

Consider the fact that there are many others like the little match girl out there. Some are young, some are old, and they are of both sexes. Eventually, Heavenly Father will take them back to His presence with love. But, until that day, they need someone to seek them out, and give them the warmth and love they require while on the earth. Decide how you can help someone in need. Then place a box of matches on a shelf where you will see it to remind you of what you will do to help.

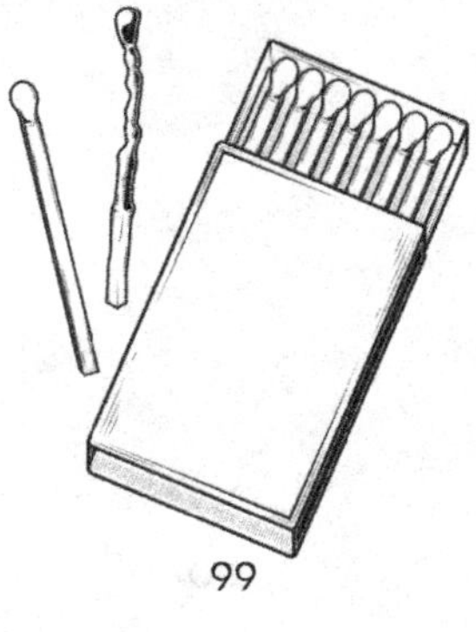

77. Lights & People

Drive around to see the Christmas lights and decorations. Contemplate that the people in those homes have a yearning for God's love and are reaching out to experience the Spirit of Christmas. Consider the following scripture as you commit to doing your part to make that happen in as many lives as you can.

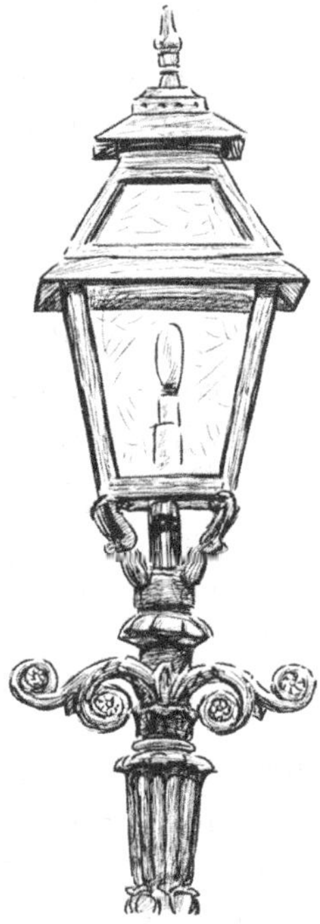

When I consider thy heavens, the work of thy fingers,
The moon and the stars, which thou hast ordained;
What is man, that thou art mindful of him?
And the son of man, that thou visitest him?
For thou hast made him a little lower than the angels,
And hast crowned him with glory and honor.

—Psalms 8: 3–5

Decide how you might expand the influence of the Spirit of Christ through your efforts. Sir Harry Lauder used to tell of an old lamplighter in a small Scottish community. When dusk would come, the old man would make the rounds with his ladder and light each street lamp. After a while, the lamplighter disappeared into the night. But Sir Harry said, "I could always tell which way he had gone because of the lamps he lighted."

78. Make a Christmas Treasure Box

Each Christmas, save one or more items as a reminder of something special from that Christmas. Keep them in a treasure box, and add to it each year. A day or two after Christmas, select new items to add, and then go through the older items to remember again the blessings of the past. As the Christmas season comes to its close, enjoy the afterglow as you do the embers of a campfire at the end of a pleasant evening.

Just as with many other things,
memories keep better in containers.
Anything can be used to keep a memory fresh.
It must merely be told to do so.

—Brent R. Evans

79. Christmas is a Time . . .

On a white board, sheet of card-stock, or poster paper, write *Christmas is a Time . . .*. Write quotes, feelings, etc. about Christmas below. Invite friends and family who visit to add their thoughts and feelings. Consider the words that have been written and make this Christmas reflect the best of those thoughts expressed.

For in thee, O Lord, do I hope.

—Psalms 38: 15

Be kindly affectioned one to another with brotherly love;
in honour preferring one another . . .
fervent in spirit; serving the Lord;
Rejoicing in hope; patient in tribulation;
continuing instant in prayer.

—Romans 12: 10–12

80. Reminders of Powerful Stories

Find objects to remind you of any story that has the power to generate loving and righteous emotions. Place a crutch in the corner of the room as a reminder of Tiny Tim's crutch from A Christmas Carol. Or, place a comb and a watch chain on a shelf to bring to mind The Gift of the Magi.

Read the following true pioneer story to see whether it affects you as it has me. Then consider whether a red shawl placed somewhere in your room might act as a reminder of parental love and the importance of having the proper perspective in our lives.

> Arthur Parker was a pioneer boy, just six years old, crossing the wide expanse on the way to Utah in a handcart company. When a sudden thunderstorm struck, there was a great hurry to make camp. It was then discovered to the distress of his parents, that Arthur was missing. For two days, the company searched, but to no avail. Being able to wait no longer, the pioneers started west again. Arthur's father prepared to go back along the trail alone and search for his beloved son once more.
>
> His wife pinned a bright shawl around his shoulders, and told him, "If you find our boy dead, wrap him in this shawl to bury him, but if you find him alive, wave this shawl as a flag when you approach me that I might know as early as possible that our son is alive." At sundown, three days later, she and her other children saw in the distance the father waving the red shawl.
>
> —Adapted from *Handcarts to Zion* by LeRoy and Ann Hafen

81. A Soft Bed for Baby Jesus

Set up a nativity scene, but wait until Christmas morning to place the baby Jesus in His manger. During the holiday, explain to your family that you will make the manger bed soft for Him by putting one piece of straw into the manger for each good deed you do. Let your family all work together doing good deeds to make the manger bed really soft before Christmas morning.

O holy Child of Bethlehem, Descend to us, we pray;
Cast out our sin, and enter in, Be born in us to-day.
We hear the Christmas angels The great glad tidings tell:
Oh, come to us, abide with us, Our Lord Emmanuel!

—Phillips Brooks

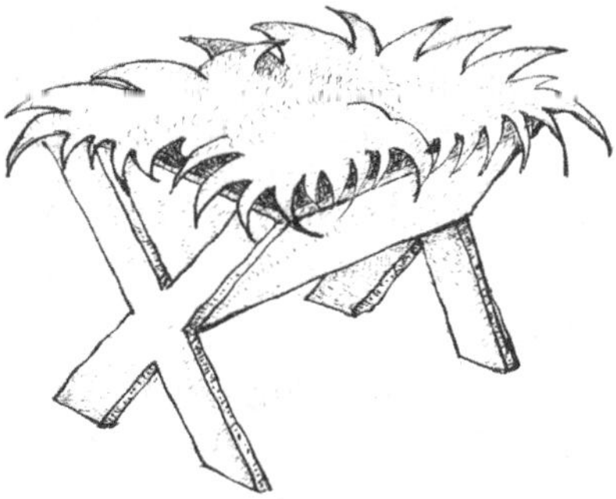

82. Christmas Symbols Basket

Find a container to use as your Christmas Symbols Basket, and then include in it a small object representing each of the items in the list below.

Present these symbols to your family, explaining the meanings of each one, and then place the basket near the Christmas tree as a reminder.

Children will love the challenge of identifying each symbol and its meaning.

Come up with new symbols to include each year.

- The Star. The heavenly sign of the Savior's birth and the shining hope of mankind.
- The Color Red. The first color of Christmas, symbolizing the Savior's sacrifice for all.
- The Fir Tree. The evergreen tree's color is the second color of Christmas, showing everlasting life as its needles point heavenward.
- The Bell. The bell ringing out to guide lost sheep back to the fold, signifying that all are precious in the eyes of the Lord.
- The Candle. The candle is the mirror of starlight, reflecting our thanks for the star of Bethlehem.
- The Gift Bow. The bow is tied together as we should all be tied—in bonds of goodwill for each other.
- The Candy Cane. Representing the shepherds' crook, which is used to bring lambs back into the fold—a reminder that we are all our brothers' and sisters' keepers.
- The Wreath. The wreath is a symbol of the eternal nature of God's love—having no beginning and no end.
- The Lamb. The baby lamb reminds us that Jesus Christ is the Lamb of God, Savior of us all.

83. Discover Your Special Gifts

Contemplate your unique gifts and talents and how they may benefit others. Then make a plan for sharing them with friends and family.

Each of us has a gift which is peculiar to him,
and which worthily used will be a gift also to his race.

—Ruskin

Now there are diversities of gifts, but the same Spirit . . .
For to one is given by the Spirit the word of wisdom;
to another the word of knowledge by the same Spirit;
To another the working of miracles;
to another prophecy;
to another discerning of spirits;
to another divers kinds of tongues;
to another the interpretation of tonques:
But all these worketh that one
and the selfsame Spirit,
dividing to every man severally as he will.

—1 Corinthians 12: 4, 8–11

84. A Special "Merry" Day

The word merry is Old English for a special type of positive courage or joyful faith. How would you look or act if you were fully merry, feeling this kind of courage and joy? Would you radiate this feeling with smiles? Select a particular day to radiate this feeling to everyone you meet. Afterward, take some time to think about the effect this had on you and on others.

A happy man or woman is a radiant focus of goodwill,
and their entrance into a room
is as though another candle had been lighted.

—Robert Louis Stevenson

You only gave a smile
Which cost you not a thing,
And yet it made me rich
As any ancient king.
You only gave me a smile

My name you did not call,
And yet it made my day
The brightest day of all.
But smiles elicit smiles
And we each won a friend.
For something free, I'd say
That's quite a dividend.

—Perry Tanksley

85. Celebrate the Festival of Lights

During November or December, share a tradition kept by people of the Jewish faith by celebrating your faith in God during the eight days of Hanukkah, which is Hebrews for dedication.

This is a celebration that also has meaning in the Christian world. It relates to a time when a small group of faithful Jewish people resisted being forced to give up their religion. Courageous acts of heroism occurred during that time and even an event in the temple that is celebrated today as a miracle occurred after the close of what we call the Old Testament and before the birth of Christ.

Read the following account with your family, and light one of the eight candles each night of Hanukkah in remembrance of the mighty struggle that preserved their religious freedom, of the liberation of the temple, and of the miracle of the oil. Let your Jewish friends know how much you also appreciate what they are celebrating.

> The king of Syria was determined to rid Judea of any trace of their religion. He tortured and killed anyone who resisted him. In a small town near Jerusalem, an old Jewish priest named Matthias threw down the Greek idol that was placed there and called out, "Whoever is for the Lord, follow me!"
>
> Thus began a rebellion that included some of the most dramatic episodes in military history. A relatively small band of determined Jewish fighters stood off and defeated the many times larger forces of the Syrian king.
>
> In 165 BC, they recaptured the city of Jerusalem from the Syrians. The Syrians had desecrated the temple by sacrificing pigs to Greek gods there and had destroyed much of it. The faithful Jews set about to clean up, repair, and re-consecrate their beloved temple.
>
> They needed oil to light the temple's seven-branched candelabrum, which always burned. But they found only one jar of oil which was enough to last one day. Miraculously, the oil burned for eight days, until more oil could be obtained. This miracle is celebrated today as Hanukkah.

As you share the tradition of Hanukkah with your family, explain the significance of the dreidel. This is a four-sided top, traditionally used in a game that is often played after the candles are lit and gifts are exchanged. A dreidel has a Hebrew letter on each of its four sides. The letters are the first letters of Hebrew words in a phrase meaning, "A great miracle happened there." If you don't have actual dreidels, here is a modified version of the game, using a six-sided die.

Each player begins with an equal number of candies, raisins, or nuts. At the start, each player puts one candy into the center, or the pot, as an ante. Then players take turns rolling the die. Anytime a 5 or a 6 comes up, the player rolls again. If a 1 is rolled, the player does nothing. If a 2 is rolled, the player puts one candy, raisin, or nut into the pot. If a 3 is rolled, the player wins half the pot. If a 4 is rolled, the player wins the whole pot. Play continues until one player has won all the candies, raisins, or nuts. Or, you may designate that the game will be over at the end of an agreed-upon time period.

86. Loved Ones from the Past

The Christmas season is a good time for you to appreciate loved ones who have died. Visit their grave sites with family or friends. Spend some time looking at photos or other memorabilia. Then, look forward to a time of joyous reunion, as promised in the scriptures.

For friendship holds a sacred cord,
That with the fibers of my heart
Entwines so deep, so close, 'tis hard
For death's dissecting hand to part.
I feel the low responses roll
Like far-off echoes of the night
And whisper softly through my soul,
I would not be forgotten quite.

—Eliza R. Snow—pioneer poet

I am the resurrection, and the life:
he that believeth in me,
though he were dead,
yet shall he live:
And whosoever liveth and believeth in me
shall never die.

—John 11: 25–26

87. Christmas & the Winter Solstice

In December, in the Northern Hemisphere, the days become ever shorter, and the nights become longer. Then comes the winter solstice on December 21, when the sun seems to have a rebirth as the days start to grow longer once again. Connect this event with Christmas as an example of rebirth.

Behold, I make all things new.
— Revelation 21: 5

88. Happy Holiday Candy Wreath

Make a candy wreath to hang on a wall or your front door during the twelve days before Christmas. You can do this by tying individually wrapped pieces of candy to a wire wreath frame or to a coat hanger bent into a circle. You will need to use very fine wire to tie each candy onto the wreath.

For each piece of candy, take a six-inch strand of the fine wire, bend it in half, and wrap this bend around the tail of the plastic candy wrapper, twisting the wire close to the wrapper's tail until secure. Then begin to attach each candy to the wire frame. Continue attaching candies, until the frame is completely full. You can tie a pair of scissors to a ribbon and hang them from the top of the wreath. You can also place a bow at the top, along with a sign saying Merry Christmas.

Each evening during the 12 days before Christmas, gather your family and visitors or friends around the wreath and have them take turns telling why they are thankful for Christmas, what Christmas means to them, or what about their family or friends makes them happy. After each person shares, the group tells that person to "Have a happy holiday candy." They may then cut off and enjoy a piece of candy from the wreath.

Later, write down the comments in your Christmas book so that they may be saved and treasured in coming years. Your candy wreath can also be hung on your front door for visitors to cut a candy off as best wishes are expressed. Be sure to replenish the candies if you have a lot of guests!

The best and most beautiful things in the world
cannot be seen or even touched.
They must be felt with the heart.

—Helen Keller

89. Twelve Days of Christmas

Ask each family member to hang a Christmas stocking beginning twelve days before Christmas. Place a small treat or gift in each one at night to be discovered and enjoyed each morning.

Or assign each family member to act as a Santa Claus to another member of the family, giving each the responsibility of taking care of that other person's stocking. The trick with this activity is to keep who each person is assigned to a secret and make each day a little extra special for everyone.

Parents without children at home can act as Santa to each other. A single person can send a package to a loved one containing twelve wrapped items to be opened each of the twelve days before Christmas.

By this shall all men know
that ye are my disciples,
if ye have love one to another.

—John 14: 35

Christmas is a beautiful dream
you can experience best when wide awake.

—Brent R. Evans

90. Baby's First Christmas

Appreciate and pay particular attention to babies during the Christmas season.

Make it a special day for that baby and its family by giving a special ornament or gift signifying the importance of the day.

Observe and appreciate the tender love and care given by the mother and father and ponder on the care Jesus received in the loving arms of Mary and Joseph.

Recall that the "little ones" are precious in our Savior's sight.

Hang up the baby's stocking:
Be sure you don't forget—
The dear little dimpled darling!
She ne'er saw Christmas yet;
But I've told her all about it,
And she opened her big blue eyes,
And I'm sure she understood it,
She looked so funny and wise.
Dear! What a tiny stocking!
It doesn't take much to hold
Such little pink toes as baby's
Away from the frost and cold.
But then, for the baby's Christmas
It will never do at all;
Why, Santa wouldn't be looking
For anything half so small.
I know what will do for the baby,
I've thought of the very best plan—
I'll borrow a stocking of grandma,
The longest that ever I can;
And you'll hang it by mine, dear mother,
Right here in the corner, so!
And write a letter to Santa,
And fasten it on to the toe.

Write, "This is the baby's stocking
That hangs in the corner here:
You never have seen her, Santa,
For she only came this year;
But she's just the blessedest baby—
And now, before you go,
Just cram her stockings with goodies,
From the top clean down to the toe.

—Anonymous

91. Collect & Memorize Christmas Songs

Select one new Christmas song each year. Memorize the words, learn the singing parts, and discuss fully the meaning and message with your family. If possible, find out the story behind the song.

The words for *Silent Night* were written on Christmas Eve in 1818, by Joseph Mohr, an assistant priest in an obscure village in Austria. The organ of his small church was broken, and Father Mohr decided to write a new hymn as a substitute for the usual organ music. Franz Gruber, the organist, wrote the music for the song to be accompanied by guitar. It is now the most sung of all Christmas carols.

Silent night! Holy night!
All is calm, all is bright;
Round yon Virgin Mother and Child,
Holy Infant so tender and mild:
Sleep in heavenly peace,
Sleep in heavenly peace.

Silent night! Holy night!
Darkness flies, all is light;
Shepherds hear the angels sing:
Alleluia! Hail the King!
Christ the Saviour is born.

Silent night! Holy night!
Guiding Star, lend thy light!
See the Eastern Wise Men bring
Gifts and homage to our King!
Christ the Saviour is born,
Christ the Saviour is born.

Silent night! Holy night!
Wondrous Star, lend thy light!
With the angels let us sing
Alleluia to our King!
Christ the Saviour is born.

92. A Christmas Toast

A toast is when we drink to some person, thing, or event in celebration. The term toast originated from the early custom of putting spiced toast into a special drink.

At the end of Christmas Day, prepare special strips of cinnamon toast and glasses of apple cider or some other special drink. Ask each person to offer a toast for the coming year and a wish and a commitment that the Spirit of Christ may continue to fill your lives all year long.

May each Christmas, as it comes,
find us more and more like Him
who at this time became a little child,
for our sake; more simple-minded,
more humble, more affectionate,
more resigned, more happy,
more full of God.

—John Henry Newman

93. The Spirit of Christmas Past

If the Spirit of Christmas Past visited you, like he did Scrooge, what things would he show you? Reflect back on the past year, and see if there are things you would like to change or correct during the coming year.

Not in the clamor of the crowded street,
Not in the shouts and plaudits of the throng,
But in ourselves, are triumph and defeat.

—Henry Wadsworth Longfellow

94. Tablecloth Christmas Story

Use a flat sheet or a large piece of cloth to make a tablecloth Christmas story. Draw on the cloth with colored permanent markers or paints. Start at one side of the sheet, and go around it, drawing pictures to tell the Christmas story.

And there were in the same country shepherds
abiding in the field, keeping watch over their flock by night.
And, lo, the angel of the Lord came upon them,
and the glory of the Lord shone round about them:
and they were sore afraid.
And the angel said unto them,
Fear not: for, behold,
I bring you good tidings of great joy,
which shall be to all people.

—Luke 2: 8–10

95. Build Fun Memories

The possibilities for new family traditions include almost anything that catches on and is either meaningful or fun. Ask your family what they would like to try, to see if you can come up with a few unique traditions of your own. Unique family traditions help to strengthen familial bonds and build lasting memories.

In our house, for example, our unique tradition was the challenge that my children had of wrestling me out of bed on Christmas morning, which had to be done before anyone was allowed to go in where the Christmas tree and presents were. Year after year, the struggle became more intense and creative. I even had to resort to such tricks as these:

- Locking my bedroom door.
- Using water guns to hold them off.
- Tying myself to the bed.
- Putting ice cubes down the backs of their pajamas.
- Hiding, and leaving a series of notes from the Grinch, who had supposedly kidnapped me, with clues for where to look.
- Placing newspapers over the bedroom windows, and then turning the clocks back several hours so that the children would think it wasn't morning yet.
- Hiding inside one of the large, wrapped presents. When my children became too big, the grandchildren took over.

96. Gingerbread Houses

Decorating gingerbread houses is a really fun tradition. Nothing is better than the aroma of fresh gingerbread in your home at Christmas time, but it can also be done with graham crackers to simplify the process.

Start with a sure foundation, a firm piece of cardboard or other material upon which to build. You can teach about the strength and importance of building our foundation on Christ.

Therefore whosoever heareth these sayings of mine,
and doeth them, I will liken him unto a wise man,
which built his house upon a rock:
And the rain descended, and the floods came,
and the winds blew, and beat upon that house;
and it fell not: for it was founded upon a rock.
And every one that heareth these sayings of mine,
and doeth them not, shall be likened unto a foolish man,
which built his house upon the sand:
And the rain descended, and the floods came,
and the winds blew, and beat upon that house;
and it fell: and great was the fall of it.

Matthew 7: 24-27.

In my Father's house are many mansions:
if it were not so, I would have told you.
I go to prepare a place for you.

—John 14: 2

97. As Jesus Would See You

Consider what Jesus Christ sees and feels as He looks at you and your life. Contemplate the love He has for you. If you were the only other person who would ever live on this earth, He would still have come to save you.

Imagine His pain and concern for some of your actions. But remind yourself that He sees also what you can become if you will follow His teachings. He is your advocate always and is totally committed to your success in reaching the kingdom of God. Consider the meanings of the following verse and quotation, and then try to remember the Savior's commitment each time you close your prayers in His name:

Wherefore he is able also to save them to the uttermost
that come unto God by him,
seeing he ever liveth to make intercession for them.

—Hebrews 7: 25

So now, since we have been made right in God's sight
by faith in his promises,
we can have real peace with him
because of what Jesus Christ our Lord has done for us.
For because of our faith,
he has brought us into this place of highest privilege
where we now stand,
and we confidently and joyfully look forward
to actually becoming all that God
has had in mind for us to be.

—Romans 5: 1–2

(Paraphrased from *The Children's Living Bible*)

98. Raise Your Ebenezer This Christmas

The word Ebenezer in Hebrews means stone of help. The Israelites, under attack by the Philistines, asked Samuel to cry unto the Lord for deliverance.

And Samuel took a sucking lamb,
and offered it for a burnt offering wholly unto the Lord:
and Samuel cried unto the Lord for Israel;
and the Lord heard him.
The Lord came to their aid
and they were rescued from the hands of their enemies.
Then Samuel took a stone,
and set it between Mizpeh and Shen,
and called the name of it Ebenezer,
saying, Hitherto hath the Lord helped us.

—1 Samuel 9–12

When we remember the things the Lord has done in our lives, we are raising our Ebenezer. Remembering our spiritual experiences, miracles, and blessings given to us by the Lord has great value in our own lives and to our posterity. Remembering that the Lord was with us increases our faith in Him and assures us that we are loved by the Savior of the world and that we are not alone. He will always come to us and provide for us if we are willing to turn our hearts to Him.

Look for these experiences during the Christmas season. Seek for opportunities to feel the spirit. Pray that you will be able to see the Lord's hand in your life and in the lives of your loved ones. Find a stone and write the words "Hitherto hath the Lord helped us" and place it on your mantle to remind you that the Lord is with you and watching over your loved ones. Reflect often on these experiences and you will have peace.

Peace I leave with you,
my peace I give unto you:
not as the world giveth,
give I unto you.
Let not your heart be troubled,
neither let it be afraid.

—John 14:27

Come Thou Fount of Every Blessing

Come thou fount of every blessing
Tune my heart to sing thy grace.
Streams of mercy never ceasing
Call for songs of loudest praise.
Teach me some melodious sonnet
Sung by flaming tongues above
I'll praise the mount I'm fixed upon it
Mount of thy redeeming love.

Here I raise my Ebenezer
Hither by thy help I come.
And I hope by thy good pleasure
Safely to arrive at home
Jesus sought me when a stranger
Wondering from the fold of God
He, to rescue me from danger
Interposed His precious blood.

O to grace how great a debtor
Daily I'm constrained to be!
Let thy goodness like a fetter,
Bind my wandering heart to thee
Prone to wander Lord I feel it,
Prone to leave the God I love
Here's my heart, O take and seal it,
Seal it for thy courts above.

Lyrics: Robert Robinson
Music: John Wyeth

99. Christmas Alphabet

Along the left side of a piece of paper, write the letters of the alphabet with one letter on each line. Then write down what each letter stands for in a Christmas way. This can be done on poster paper and placed on your Christmas Wall. This example from an unknown author will help you, but it will be more special for you to create your own.

A is for Animals who shared the stable.
B is for the Babe with their manger for His cradle.
C is for the Carols so blithe and so gay.
D is for December, the twenty-fifth day.
E is for Even when we're all so excited.
F is for the Fun when the tree's at last lighted.
G is the Goose which you all know is fat.
H is for the Holly you stick in your hat.
I is for the Ivy that clings to the wall.

J is for Jesus, the cause of it all.
K is for the Kindness begot by this feast.
L is the Light shining way in the east.
M is for the Mistletoe, all green and white.
N is for the Noels we sing Christmas night.
O is for the Oxen, the first to adore Him.
P is for the Presents Wise Men laid before Him.
Q is for the Queerness that this should have been
near two thousand years before you were seen.
R is for the Reindeer leaping the roofs.
S is for the Stockings that Santa Claus stuffs.
T is for the Toys, the Tinsel, the Tree.
U is for Us—the whole family.
V is for Visitors bringing us cheer.
W is Welcome to the happy New Year.
X Y Z bother me! All I can say is,
This is the end of my Christmas lay.
So now to you all, wherever you be,
A merry, merry Christmas, and many may you see!

100. Memorize the Christmas Story in Luke

Make the scriptures come to life for you and your family by memorizing the beautiful Christmas account of Christ's birth found in chapter 2 of Luke. Then, instead of merely reading the account, declare these glad tidings as if you were there and reporting to your loved ones what you saw. The spirit will whisper to your family the greatness of this event.

And it came to pass in those days,
that there went out a decree from Cæsar Augustus,
that all the world should be taxed.
And all went to be taxed, every one into his own city.
And Joseph also went up from Galilee,
out of the city of Nazareth, into Judæa,
unto the city of David, which is called Bethlehem;
(because he was of the house and lineage of David:)
to be taxed with Mary his espoused wife, being great with child.
And so it was, that, while they were there,
the days were accomplished that she should be delivered.
And she brought forth her firstborn son,
and wrapped him in swaddling clothes,
and laid him in a manger;
because there was no room for them in the inn.
And there were in the same country shepherds
abiding in the field, keeping watch over their flock by night.
And, lo, the angel of the Lord came upon them,
and the glory of the Lord shone round about them:
and they were sore afraid.
And the angel said unto them,
Fear not: for, behold, I bring you good tidings of great joy,
which shall be to all people.
For unto you is born this day in the city of David a Saviour,
which is Christ the Lord.
And this shall be a sign unto you;
Ye shall find the babe wrapped in swaddling clothes,
lying in a manger.

And suddenly there was with the angel
a multitude of the heavenly host praising God, and saying,
Glory to God in the highest,
and on earth peace,
good will toward men.
And it came to pass,
as the angels were gone away from them into heaven,
the shepherds said one to another,
Let us now go even unto Bethlehem,
and see this thing which is come to pass,
which the Lord hath made known unto us.
And they came with haste,
and found Mary, and Joseph, and the babe lying in a manger.
And when they had seen it,
they made known abroad the saying
which was told them concerning this child.
And all they that heard it wondered at those things
which were told them by the shepherds.
But Mary kept all these things,
and pondered them in her heart.
And the shepherds returned,
glorifying and praising God for all the things
that they had heard and seen,
as it was told unto them.

—Luke 2:1-20

101. Give Gifts of Forgiveness

There is probably no greater gift than forgiveness. In fact, the word forgive means *super give*. Christ came to be our Savior. He came to pay the ransom for the sins of everyone who has lived, who lives now, and who will live upon the Earth. What better way to honor Him and His mission here on Earth than to give the gift of forgiveness to others or even to ourselves.

The best way to forgive a person is to serve them. Do little things throughout the season, even if only done anonymously, for the person you need to forgive.

Love your enemies, bless them that curse you,
do good to them that hate you,
and pray for them which despitefully use you,
and persecute you.

—Matthew 5: 44

If you are having difficulty finding forgiveness for yourself, go to the Lord in prayer. Repent means to turn in a new direction. Turn your life toward Christ and He will help you to know that your past mistakes are behind you.

Come now, and let us reason together, saith the Lord:
though your sins be as scarlet, they shall be as white as snow;
though they be red like crimson, they shall be as wool.

—Isaiah 1:8

102. Wassailing

The tradition of wassailing dates back to the Middle Ages. The word Wassail was an Anglo Saxon greeting meaning be thou hale or in good health. It was a reciprocal exchange between the feudal lords and the peasants. This was not considered the same as begging because the peasants would initiate the charitable exchange. Peasants, often children, would go door to door offering a drink from their wassail bowl and the lords of the manor would exchange greetings with them and send them off with gifts. Wassail later became a toast and wassailing gradually turned into Christmas Caroling where the participants were often given treats to reward them for their songs, such as figgy pudding.

Have special gifts or treats ready, as a thank you, to hand out when someone offers you a kindness or when carolers may come to your door. Perhaps someone in need will offer a service such as washing your car for which you can give generously. You can reward family members with a small gift and note expressing appreciation for their positive contributions to the family.

Here We Come a Wassailing

Here we come a-wassailing
Among the leaves so green;
Here we come a-wand'ring
So fair to be seen.
Love and joy come to you,
And to you your wassail too;
And God bless you and send you a Happy New Year
And God send you a Happy New Year.

We are not daily beggars
That beg from door to door;
But we are neighbours' children,
Whom you have seen before.

We have got a little purse
Of stretching leather skin;
We want a little of your money
To line it well within.
Bring us out a table
And spread it with a cloth;
Bring us out a mouldy cheese,
And some of your Christmas loaf.

God bless the master of this house
Likewise the mistress too,
And all the little children
That round the table go.

Good master and good mistress,
While you're sitting by the fire,
Pray think of us poor children
Who are wandering in the mire.

And God bless you and send you a Happy New Year
And God send you a Happy New Year.

103. Christmas Kindness Jar

Children have a natural sense of enjoyment when they are given the opportunity to be helpers. Encourage their desire to show kindness to others during the Christmas season with a Kindness Jar. Decorate and label a clear mason jar. Purchase a variety of brightly colored pom poms from your craft store and explain that these are warm fuzzies. A warm fuzzy is the feeling we get when we are kind and make someone else happy. Each time your child shows kindness to another, have them choose and place a "warm fuzzy" in the jar. Have a small box or bag the child can draw from each day of the Christmas season with simple acts of kindness for them to perform. These should be easy enough for the child to accomplish on their own and feel successful. Encourage the child's own efforts to come up with their own ideas of love and service.

Here are some ideas:

- Draw a picture of a Christmas tree and give it to someone to make them smile.
- Make someone a peanut butter sandwich.
- Make someone's bed in the morning.
- Call grandparents and tell them that you love them.
- Feed the birds.
- Paint a picture on a rock and leave it for someone to find.
- Read a book with someone.
- Make up a game for your family to play.
- Help make dinner.
- Donate a toy to a child in need or the fire department.
- Share a talent you have with the family.
- Leave a kind note for someone.
- Leave some pennies on the sidewalk with the heads side up for others to find. Say a special prayer for someone.
- Have a day of no complaining.

- Smile at five people today.
- Tell a joke to make someone laugh.
- Pick up ten things and put them away.
- Share a favorite toy.
- Help water the plants.
- Clean your room without being asked.
- Hide a surprise in a family member's room and let them have fun trying to find it.
- Make a new friend.
- Give someone a great big hug!
- Find some clothes that don't fit you anymore to give to someone else.
- Ask someone what their favorite color is and draw or paint a picture for them using only that color.
- Offer to scratch someone's back.
- Write (or have someone help you write) something you like about each family member and share it with the family.

104. Show Gratitude for the First Gift of Christmas

For God so loved the world,
that he gave his only begotten Son,
that whosoever believeth in him should not perish,
but have everlasting life.
For God sent not his Son into the world to condemn the world;
but that the world through him might be saved.

—John 3: 16

This scripture pierces the heart as we contemplate the love and mercy God the Father has for each of us; enough to put a plan in place where He would send His son to live among us, teach us how to love one another, heal us, and pay ransom for our sins so that we can find joy and peace and one day return to His, our Father's presence.

And this is life eternal, that they might know thee
the only true God, and Jesus Christ, whom thou hast sent.

—John 17:3

Christ came to teach us of the Father, to show us by His loving example the things our Heavenly Father would do if He were physically among us. Feeding the hungry, healing the sick, blessing the little children, and desiring us to become the best versions of ourselves, all the loving and merciful acts Christ performed here in mortality were showing us the ways and the true nature of the Father.

Then answered Jesus and said unto them,
Verily, verily, I say unto you,
The Son can do nothing of himself,
but what he seeth the Father do:
for what things soever he doeth,
these also doeth the Son likewise.

—John 5:19

This perfect Son not only pointed us toward God, but beautifully demonstrated His own devotion, honor, love, and submissiveness to the Father throughout His ministry. Let us follow His example and spend more time on our knees this season expressing our humble gratitude to our Heavenly King for the precious gift of His Son. Let us strive to become better acquainted with Him and to know and feel His great love for us. Then let us love one another.

He that loveth not knoweth not God; for God is love.
In this was manifested the love of God toward us,
because that God sent his only begotten Son into the world,
that we might live through him.
Herein is love, not that we loved God,
but that he loved us, and sent his Son
to be the propitiation for our sins.
Beloved, if God so loved us,
we ought also to love one another.

—1 John 4: 8-11

105. Love Thy Neighbor

Thou shalt love the Lord thy God with all thy heart,
and with all thy soul, and with all thy mind.
This is the first and great commandment.
And the second is like unto it,
Thou shalt love thy neighbour as thyself.

—Matthew 22:37-39

Christmas provides many wonderful opportunities to get to know our neighbors better. Invite them over on a cold evening for some simple hot chocolate and visiting. Greet them by name when you see them. Do simple acts of service for them, such as bring their newspaper to their porch or pull their garbage can back into place. Offer to help if you see them working on a project outside.

And, behold, a certain lawyer stood up, and tempted him,
saying, Master, what shall I do to inherit eternal life?
He said unto him, What is written in the law? How readest thou?
And he answering said,
Thou shalt love the Lord thy God with all thy heart,
and with all thy soul, and with all thy strength,
and with all thy mind; and thy neighbour as thyself.
And he said unto him,
Thou hast answered right: this do, and thou shalt live.
But he, willing to justify himself, said unto Jesus,
And who is my neighbour?
And Jesus answering said,
A certain man went down from Jerusalem to Jericho,
and fell among thieves, which stripped him of his raiment,
and wounded him, and departed, leaving him half dead.
And by chance there came down a certain priest that way:
and when he saw him, he passed by on the other side.
And likewise a Levite, when he was at the place,
came and looked on him, and passed by on the other side.
But a certain Samaritan, as he journeyed, came where he was:
and when he saw him, he had compassion on him,
And went to him, and bound up his wounds, pouring in oil and wine,
and set him on his own beast,and brought him to an inn, and took care of him.

And on the morrow when he departed,
he took out two pence, and gave them to the host, and said unto him,
Take care of him; and whatsoever thou spendest more,
when I come again, I will repay thee.
Which now of these three, thinkest thou,
was neighbour unto him that fell among the thieves?
And he said, He that shewed mercy on him.
Then said Jesus unto him, Go, and do thou likewise.

—Luke 10: 25 37

There is an interesting bit of background to the story of the Good Samaritan, which Jesus also used to teach His followers about service. Recall that a man lay wounded on the road. Going up the hill toward Jerusalem, a priest saw him but walked on the other side of the road and passed him by. The priest would have been on his way to the temple to take a one-week turn serving there. Because of the very large number of priests, this opportunity would have come only twice each year for him. We can discover part of this particular priest's motivation.

He that toucheth the dead body of any man
shall be unclean seven days.

—Numbers 19: 11

In other words, if this priest had investigated and had found that the man on the side of the road was dead, or if the man happened to die during the priest's ministrations, the priest would be unable to serve in the temple and would have to wait for six more months for that special opportunity to come again. This story should remind us to always make time to do the service that the Lord would really desire of us.

We may at times need to get out of our mindsets of even the good things we do and consider if there are other better needs Christ would want us to fill just laying by the wayside.

106. The Present of Presence

Look back at what you remember most from past Christmases growing up. Was it the gifts, or the interactions you had with family and loved ones? Remember that it is the time set aside and spent together that means the most. Take time to really be present and create valuable moments that will be cherished forever. Encourage quality time spent with grandparents and other relatives so that relationships can grow and flourish.

The best of all gifts around any Christmas tree:
the presence of a happy family all wrapped up in each other.

—Burton Hill

107. Yule Log

The burning of the Yule log is wonderful tradition that has been passed down from generation to generation and now it can be yours to enjoy. Even getting a tree log and bringing it to your home was treated with so much respect that villagers who saw it pass by would tip their hats. Your Yule log may have been growing in the forest for a hundred years or so, during which time it has been actively soaking in the energy, nutrients, and warmth of the sun. Upon burning the Yule log, all of that energy, warmth, and light, along with the spirit of goodness and happiness are released into your home and hearts of those basking in its glow.

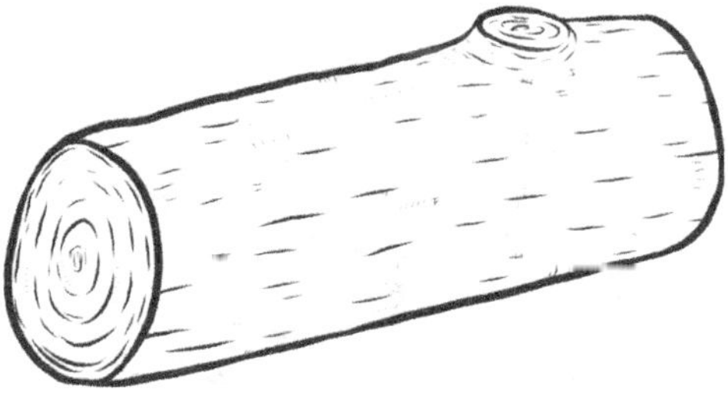

108. What Would Jesus Do?

Display the words, What would Jesus do? in a picture frame and hang it in your home as a reminder to follow the lead of Christ and do what He would do in any situation.

109. Dinner Table Devotionals

Busy schedules make regular family dinners a difficult task. This is an important time, however, for connecting with family members. Make having dinner together at the table a priority each night. Use dinner table devotionals to grow closer to God as a family. Discuss gospel topics or share an inspirational quote, story, or scripture. Invite family members to share their own thoughts and see where the conversation leads.

And these words, which I command thee this day,
shall be in thine heart:
And thou shalt teach them diligently unto thy children,
and shalt talk of them when thou sittest in thine house,
and when thou walkest by the way,
and when thou liest down,
and when thou risest up.

—Deuteronomy 6:6,7

110. Christ Be in My Everything

Rather than just setting aside Sundays and prayer time for the Savior, invite Him into every aspect of your life. Make Him present in your daily activities, in your work, in your play, in your dreaming, and in your planning. Invite Him in your listening, your loving, your peaceful moments, and your troubles. Invite Christ in your everything and you will always have His spirit with you.

111. Gifts of the Magi

Give three gifts to each person, each gift correlating to one of the gifts the wise men brought to young Jesus.

One gift represents gold. This should be whatever gift that the receiver wants the most. Keep in mind that this does not necessarily mean that this must be the most expensive gift, just the most desired.

Another gift represents frankincense. Frankincense is a holy incense used in the ancient temples. For this category, the gift would be something spiritual in nature. This could range from an inspirational book to an event such as a hike into a secluded spot to ponder. The rule of thumb for this gift is that it is a gift that would bring the receiver closer to God.

The third gift represents Myrrh. Myrrh is used in many forms but all of them revolve around dressing or preparing the physical body. For this gift, you could do something that the receiver can wear. Again, feel free to be creative in how you go about doing this and remember that it does not need to be an expensive item

112. Christmas Eve in Bethlehem

Shut out the bustle of the season and turn off the modern world and take your family back to a sacred night in Bethlehem. Hush the Christmas to do lists and last minute holiday preparations and concentrate solely on the scene of a rustic manger in a humble stable.

Lay a quilt out on the floor, gather your family close, light a few candles, and turn off the lights. Enjoy a simple meal by the candlelight's glow that resembles what people may have eaten during the time of Christ's Birth; such as nuts, dried fruits, unleavened or naan bread, lentils or bean soup.

Share tidings of comfort and joy as each expresses their love for the Savior of the World and the thoughts that have touched them personally through the Christmas season.

As you read about Mary and Joseph's journey to Bethlehem, the shepherds abiding in the fields, the angels praising God, and the wise men following the star, have a special reenactment of the events of Christ's birth with family members playing each part.

Give each member of the family a slip of paper and something to write with. Spend some quiet time as each person decides on a gift or gifts they would like to give to the Savior during the year. It might be breaking a bad habit or finding new ways to serve or anything that would bring us closer to Christ.

Write these on the slips of paper and place them, folded with names written on the outside, into a small box such as the wise man might present to the Lord and place it somewhere where it can be kept all year.

Next year during your Christmas Eve in Bethlehem, return the slips of paper to their owners and leave time for pondering. New "gifts" to give Christ are written on new slips of paper or the old slips may be placed back in, if it is felt they need to be worked on a little longer.

Together, sing a few cherished and sacred Christmas Carols as the Spirit directs. Remember the feelings you have as you invite Christ into your home.

Where meek souls will receive Him still, the dear Christ enters in.

113. Choose a Christmas Theme for Next Year

Decide on a Christmas theme for next Christmas so you will have an entire year to ponder and pray. If you are doing this individually, try reviewing scriptures about Christ's birth before making your decision on a theme. If you are doing it with your family or friends as a group, discuss various ideas before making a group decision.

Write your theme in a paragraph with supporting examples and scriptures. Then attach it to the top of your main calendar, or post it in a prominent place so that it may act as a reminder to everyone participating. As you make this a tradition every year, the time you spend selecting the new theme will become a very special occasion.

The Spirit of the Lord God is upon me;
because the Lord hath anointed me
to preach good tidings unto the meek;
he hath sent me to bind up the brokenhearted,
to proclaim liberty to the captives,
and the opening of the prison to them that are bound;
To proclaim the acceptable year of the Lord
to comfort all that morn;
to appoint unto them that mourn in Zion,
o give unto them beauty for ashes,
the oil of joy for mourning,
the garment of praise for the spirit of heaviness;
that they might be called trees of righteousness,
the planting of the Lord,
that he might be glorified.

—Isaiah 61: 1–3

114. New Year Missions, Goals, & Promises

You may want to have your Christmas season end on New Year's Day. You can help your family continue to seek and feel the Spirit of Christ by inviting them to write down mission statements, goals, and covenants they are making with the Savior for the new year.

Forgetting those things which are behind
and reaching forth unto those things which are before,
I press toward the mark
or the prize of the high calling of God in Christ Jesus.

—Philippians 3: 13

To every man there openeth
A way, and ways and a way.
And the high soul climbs the high way
And the low soul climbs the low,
And in between, on the misty flats,
The rest drift to and fro.
But to every man there openeth
A high way and a low:
And every man decideth
Which way his soul shall go.

—John Oxenham

And above all, have joy in your world this year and every year of your lives! Consider the gift of profound joy that becomes yours by greeting each day with Merry Christmas joy.

Joy to the World, the Lord has come!
Let earth receive her King;
Let every heart prepare Him room,
And Heaven and nature sing,
And Heaven and nature sing,
And Heaven, and Heaven, and nature sing.

The movie, *Chariots of Fire,* tells the story of Eric Liddell, a Scottish athlete, who inspired everyone when he won an Olympic Gold medal in track at the 1924 Summer Olympics in Paris. He said, "I believe God made me for a purpose, but he also made me fast. And when I run, I feel His pleasure."

Couldst thou in vision see
Thyself, the person God meant,
Thou never then would be
The person thou art, content.

—Anonymous

115. Celebrate the Feast of the Epiphany

When the Christmas lights no longer line the streets and the Christmas music stations have gone silent, many households are still celebrating Christmas up to and including the feast of the Epiphany, which is not considered the end, but the culmination of the Christmas season. An epiphany is an experience of a sudden and striking realization. The Epiphany refers to a realization that Jesus is the Son of God. It is celebrated January 6th in commemoration of the arrival of the Magi to the Christ child.

The three gifts the Magi, or Wise Men, presented to the young Jesus may seem like odd selections, but the gold, frankincense and myrrh were valuable gifts fit for a King. These gifts were Heaven sent. Through these humble and wise Magi, God, knowing beforehand Herod's plan to kill the child, provided a means for which Joseph would be able to take his family and escape into Egypt. The Wise Men's gifts effectively kept the young Savior of the World safe from harm.

ABOUT BRENT R. EVANS

What I Want Most in Life

I want to make a positive difference in the lives of other people.

I want to help build an eternal family that will thoroughly enjoy each other and be a support to each other.

I want to find out about beauty and life, and to point out or share what I learn with loved ones so they don't miss out.

And, I want to create more books! Here are some that are on the way . . .

IQ BOOSTERS
Published September 2018

CHRISTMAS BOOSTERS

Published September 2018

Coming in 2019

CHARACTER BOOSTERS
SPIRITUAL BOOSTERS
PHYSICAL BOOSTERS

Made in the USA
Monee, IL
02 November 2023

45618738R00090